Dear Hasson
Warm regards
Floyd

SUCCESSFUL STRATEGIES FOR SALES MANAGERS

SUCCESSFUL STRATEGIES FOR SALES MANAGERS

A Guide To Get The Best From Salespeople

Floyd Wickman

Executive Press

High Point, North Carolina

Copyright © 1987 by Floyd Wickman Assoc., Inc.

Library of Congress Cataloging in Publication Data

ISBN 0–9399–7500–9

Published by Executive Press
806 Westchester Drive
High Point, NC 27262

Printed in the United States of America.

Second Printing

To all the managers of the world who set out to slay dragons, and ended up only stepping on a few lizards.

Or, I saw a bumper sticker the other day. It read, "Gotta hurry. There go my people, and I'm their leader."

Floyd Wickman

Contents

Preface

Managing salespeople is somewhat different from managing employees in other professions. Salespeople are self-reliant souls who are not as likely to knuckle under to management demands as other employees. If they decide they don't like the rules of one organization, they can go to work for another. The sales business is extremely competitive and, as a result, there are no shortages of jobs during average (and especially during above average) economic times.

Salespeople are extremely independent by nature. That's often why they are in the sales business in the first place. They like and very much desire the freedom that the sales profession offers. But often, this freedom can lead to their undoings. Given the option to fail (which automatically comes with independency), improperly managed salespeople often will take this option, because failing is easier than succeeding.

A salesperson generally will function no better than his or her manager. Since sales managers derive their incomes (either directly or indirectly) from the production of their salespeople, it's to their advantage to lead them correctly.

Managing a team of salespeople is no easy effort. If you've been a sales manager for any length of time at all, you'll know that I'm right. But do you know that sales managers of successful sales teams actually have easier jobs than managers of less than successful teams? The reason for this is simple: They know what they're doing, and they don't mind having fun in the process. In fact, successful sales managers know that fun is a very essential ingredient to managing a successful sales team.

If you aren't sure what steps to take to lead your sales team to success, don't feel like a failure. You've got a lot of company. Many sales managers would benefit if they would change some of their methods of managing. If you're not sure how to mix business with fun, take heart, because you're holding in your hands the book that can show you how to have the type of fun that can and will boost your sales team's production.

Of course, a minority of sales organizations in North America are faring quite well without any help. These organizations are led by sales managers who have the necessary know-how and energy to lead their sales teams to success. But that doesn't mean that the majority of struggling sales organizations are doomed to failure. These sales teams have what it takes, but they lack the leadership that it takes to succeed. They need a new leader.

That new leader can be you! There is nothing special about this leadership quality. There's nothing special about "special" sales managers. It's what they do that counts, and "special" sales managers know exactly what they're doing. That's what makes the difference.

This book can and will teach you what to do to become a successful leader. It was written for the majority of sales managers who could stand to benefit from learning the proper techniques. By following the principles set down in this book, you'll be able to build a sales team that can set company records.

LEARN TO EARN

To build or rebuild a sales team requires growth, which is simply capturing a greater percentage of the market share. Growth requires a change of energy in the team's leadership. But I've learned in my career as a real estate salesman, manager, trainer and speaker that, often, the hardest person to teach new ideas is the boss. If the boss doesn't learn new tricks of the trade, it's a good bet that the salespeople won't learn them either.

For example, as a sales consultant, I have been called periodically to diagnose various ills that kept sales organizations operating in the red. Thirty-one out of thirty-four times, I was able to increase production by at least fifty percent (the three unsuccessful cases are attributable to the sales manager vetoing my suggestions). But in twenty-nine of those thirty-one successful companies, production eventually returned to the unacceptable norm because I didn't teach the manager what I had done.

That's why I wrote this book. It contains all a sales manager needs to know to lead a successful sales team. Of course, the content is generic, because there are so many different types of sales organizations in existence. But the process of managing is the same, regardless of the product. This book offers you some techniques that come straight from the field. I've traveled enough of the continent and talked with enough sales managers to know that they work!

THE FIVE JOBS OF A MANAGER

A sales manager has five jobs—**recruit, train, direct, motivate** and **upgrade** the sales team. This book will detail each job as well as offer tips, suggestions and ideas to make you proficient at each job.

The book includes a section on how to recruit, which includes chapters on creating an attractive classified ad, a sound interviewing process, how to "sell" your company to the applicant and the secrets of hiring successful salespeople.

Although this book is generic and, as a result, would sharply curtail any material I could offer on the subject of training, I have included a chapter that offers generic training principles that are applicable and can strengthen any sales organization, regardless of the product sold.

A two-chapter section on direction includes suggestions on how to build a team and solve personality problems with individual salespeople that could threaten, if not destroy, your positive progress.

The book contains a chapter on how to motivate salespeople by staging contests designed to be fun and rewarding for both the salespeople and the company. The thirteenth chapter of the book is devoted to upgrading the status of your sales team, offering a six-step process for increasing company profits.

What's more, you'll have fun while using these techniques, because most of them are designed to make your job fun, and your salespeople's jobs as well. Fun is not just a by-product of a successful sales organization; it's an essential ingredient. The atmosphere of a sales organization makes it successful, and a successful sales organization's atmosphere must be friendly, fun and competitive. Show me an office or a company that has a friendly, fun and competitive atmosphere, and I'll show you a productive company. A sales organization with a solemn business atmosphere is light years away from its full market potential. People like to have fun. We're all just tall kids. Smart managers realize this, and they get the most from their salespeople!

How do I know this? Long before I stood behind the speaker's podium, I sat in the audience. I always wanted to know the same thing: How does the speaker know what he or she is saying?

I have a unique perspective of the sales business. I got into sales in the mid-60's, and I did very poorly for the first year. What I remember from that period in my life is how a salesperson shouldn't be managed. After a year in the sales business, I was convinced that I was a loser. But then, I changed companies and went to work for somebody who knew how to manage, and I became a success at selling. That's when I learned how a salesperson should be managed.

Preface

I subsequently became a real estate office manager, and for four years, I had one of the most successful offices in the metropolitan Detroit area. For more than a decade, I've been involved in sales training. I've taught thousands of salespeople the "how-to's" of selling, and managers the "how-to's" of recruiting, training, directing, motivating and upgrading their staffs.

Now I'm well aware that there are many management books on the market that were written by people more intelligent than I am. But when it comes to sales, I personally believe that there are very few Ph.D.'s directly in charge of managing salespeople. Most books on salespeople management seem to be heavy on philosophy and light on actual "how-to" content. Virtually all of these sales books seem to be written more for the company's chairman of the board than the sales manager.

This book is unique in that it talks directly to the sales manager. Most sales managers are former successful salespeople who have worked their way up from the ranks. Successful salespeople are everyday people who talk in everyday terms like you and me. They don't sit around and discuss theories and philosophies. They're too busy selling.

Between you and me, we can keep them selling. That should be good news for all concerned. Stick with me through the chapters of this book, and I'll show you how to **recruit, train, direct, motivate** and **upgrade** your way to success.

Section 1

GETTING A SOLID START

Strategy 1:

Form a Solid Foundation

Let's get down to business. After all, that's why you're reading this book, isn't it? You want to learn how to maximize your sales team's efforts to increase the profits generated by the business you're responsible for managing.

HAVING FUN?

Let me ask you a simple question: Do you have fun with your job? Seriously, do you regard your job as sales manager as toil and drudgery? If you do, it probably is. But it needn't be that way. The best work is the kind that is fun.

Any kind of work can be fun, provided that the worker has the proper attitude. Remember Tom Sawyer? Whitewashing the fence wasn't his idea of fun, but he was successful at convincing enough of his pals that the chore was indeed an honor and privilege for the relatively few people in the world who were talented enough to do it. Of course, he had no trouble attracting these "gifted" few people from his own neighborhood, because he knew how to communicate effectively. His description of the task appealed to their senses of challenge and fun. As a result, Tom Sawyer had fun with his work, because other people did it for him.

There's a lesson in that famous story: Successful managers can breeze through life if they can "sell" fun in exchange for work. Successful sales managers do just that; they can build their personal fortunes by making their subordinates' jobs as much fun as possible. When they do that, they, like Tom Sawyer, can reap the rewards while others do the work. In Tom's case, the rewards were finishing the job faster, more efficiently, with less personal effort and having more of the remaining day to pursue his own pastimes. Successful sales managers' rewards will be much the same, but on a grander scale. Furthermore, they'll get paid for their trouble, which, if they're smart, will be no trouble at all.

Unsuccessful sales managers usually sing the blues, because their jobs are indeed difficult. It's not very much fun when they, in addition to performing their other duties, must get out and make enough sales to keep the company solvent. This is a major problem with most sales managers; for one reason or another, they spread themselves too thinly to meet their total responsibilities. And if they don't go crazy in the process, they become insufferable grouches. Of course, no one bucks them; but no one respects them, either.

As a result, unsuccessful sales managers work harder, get more headaches and fewer rewards than their successful contemporaries. Doesn't that seem ironic?

Sales managers weren't meant to be grouches. In fact, the sales manager who knows how to have fun will not only be better respected and admired, but also will be more successful, because the sales team will be more successful. After all, unsuccessful sales managers try to intimidate to get what they want. Successful sales managers motivate salespeople to act in their own best interests, which, of course, also is in the sales manager's best interests.

Too many business people tend to maintain solemn business atmospheres because, in their estimation, business is serious business indeed. Yet, such a business is light years away from its potential, because no one in a position of leadership knows how to have on-the-job, productive fun.

If you would be a successful sales manager, you should realize that, in many ways, salespeople are little more than just tall kids. They want to have fun while they work, and the successful sales manager should know just how to create an atmosphere of fun. This book will help teach you how to do this. When you're finished reading it, you'll know how to make those who work for you have so much fun with their jobs that you shouldn't have to do anything but oversee your department and watch your bank account grow.

START OUT STRONG

First, have you ever wondered why some sales organizations seem to grow continuously, while others frantically fight to stay in the black? What do these successful businesses have that others seem to lack? Could it be a sound business plan? The right people? Strong leadership?

Actually, successful sales organizations have all three of those qualities. Surprisingly, unsuccessful sales organizations may have as many as two out of three, yet they're still unsuccessful. And the reason for that is, unfortunately, in the case of businesses, two out of three isn't enough to ensure success.

When it comes to operating a successful sales organization, all three factors must be present to compose a strong foundation for

5

the business itself. If any one is missing, or even weak, the foundation will be weak and eventually will crumble under the weight of the organization it is trying to support.

If a sales organization's foundation is weak, all the management techniques in the world won't help it. With a weak foundation, a sales organization will forever fight to stay in the black, at best, and, at worst, may wind up in bankruptcy court. Neither option sounds like very much fun.

THE MONEY TRIANGLE

I like to think of this three-part foundation as a triangle, with a dollar-sign ($) in the center. Each point of the triangle represents a footing for the foundation, and each must be solid and strong to help support the organization.

Let's review this three-part foundation:

1. *Sound business plan.* This includes market projections, company policies, job descriptions, budgets and systems of operation. A company's goals and purpose must be clearly stated in the business plan as a guide to not only the manager, but to the salespeople as well.

    Salespeople have forever been told that if they want to succeed at selling, they should write down attainable goals. If a company would be successful, its goals must be recorded. Budgets also should be included in the company plan.

    If there isn't a budget, some day, there may not be a company. I've heard managers say, "I've never gotten to the point where I could do a budget."

My reply is simple: "That's why." I'll say, "If you don't have a budget, you'll never get to the point where you can develop one."

Also, the company philosophy should be clearly detailed. Every successful corporation has a successful philosophy. One national real estate firm's philosophy is: To become successful by making our associates successful. That says it all.

2. *The right people.* This is most important. Any salesperson can sell, but your company needs salespeople who will be willing and able to work in accordance with the company's business plan. This must be determined in the interview process; if you hire a salesperson who isn't willing to work the plan, you'll either have a nonproductive person on your hands or a disruptive rebel who will challenge your every directive. You don't need either one.

3. *Strong leadership.* Successful salespeople want and need good leadership. Even with a sound business plan and the right people, the business will go down the drain if the manager puts his/her responsibilities on hold and takes an extended trip abroad. Good leadership also requires the right people. Too often, salespeople are blamed for poor production, while the real fault is with the manager. He or she simply may not have the right personality, drive, desire, background or human relation skills (in some cases, all of the preceding) to lead the staff to accomplish the company objectives.

If all three of these points to the sales organization triangle are solid, the business will be solid, also. But all three must be noticeably present before management techniques can be successfully applied.

MONEY TRIANGLE

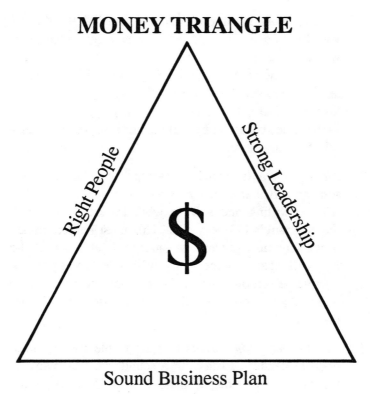

Sound Business Plan

If not, any effort you make toward revitalizing the business will be wasted or short-lived.

LET'S GET ORGANIZED

Does your sales organization have an organizational chart? For the benefit of all sales employees and, ultimately, yourself, I hope so. It's terribly important to clarify the lines of accountability and give each employee a clear idea of to whom he or she is responsible.

On the organizational chart, each employee of the business is represented by a square, which is connected by a single line to another square representing that employee's immediate supervisor.

One of the major problems of too many sales organizations is no one seems to know just who is responsible to whom. The organizational chart clarifies the chain of command. There can only be one line connecting any box to another; this means that each employee is answerable to only one superior.

Suppose, in a sales organization, a particular salesperson is responsible to several different people, such as the sales manager, the company president, the president's secretary and several vice presidents. As a result, the salesperson's box would be connected to each of those position's boxes by separate lines, which I call responsibility and authority lines.

If you make a salesperson responsible and answerable to too many people, you're going to accomplish one of three things. The salesperson either will:

—have a nervous breakdown from the strain of being accountable to too many people.

—be strangled by one of the superiors, who will become irate because the salesperson chose to neglect his or her directive in favor of a conflicting directive issued by another superior.

—make a strong statement in protest of the company's organizational structure by strangling the superior who issued the conflicting directive.

Then there is the upside down organizational chart; this is best illustrated by turning upside down a sound organizational chart. Instead of eight to ten salespeople being answerable to the manager, the manager is answerable to the salespeople, because he or she has never trained them to act independently. Consequently, the manager is figuratively pulled to pieces, caught in the crossfire of salespeople's multiple demands.

"Have you got time to work on my deal yet?" a salesperson might ask.

"No, not yet," the manager patiently replies. "I'm sorry. I'll be with you as soon as I finish with these other nine team members."

"Well, make it snappy," the salesperson says, puffing a strong sigh of impatience.

Save yourself and your employees some grief while making a strong contribution to good working conditions and office morale. Devise a sound organizational chart that links one employee with a single supervisor. The lines of responsibility and authority must be

UPSIDE-DOWN ORGANIZATIONAL FLOW CHART

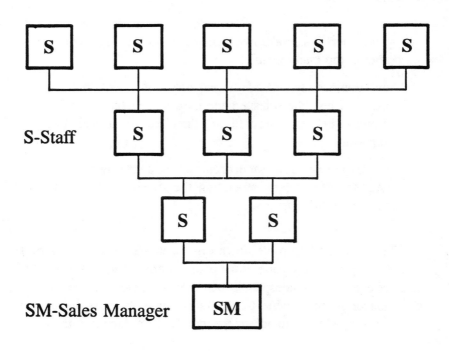

S-Staff

SM-Sales Manager

clear to obtain maximum performance from employees. If you make an employee responsible to more than one person, you will demoralize that employee, which effectively takes away his or her ability to operate at peak efficiency. You will also be costing yourself big in terms of production and retention of your sales force.

Your organizational structure will have a direct bearing on the morale and efficiency of your staff. One supervisor per person, please.

WHO'S WHO IN AN ORGANIZATION

In any sales organization, there are three key positions which are of paramount concern to a sales manager. All other positions that might exist within the company rarely, if ever, have any real bearing on the manager's duties and responsibilities. The three key positions are:

—*Owner.* This could be the president of the company, or, then again, it may not be. In any event, the top position within the organization is reserved for the investor or representative who oversees total operations, and establishes and administers company policy. This position may be directly in charge of the sales manager.

—*Salesperson.* This is one who earns a living motivating people to do things which, left to the people to decide, they wouldn't ordinarily do.

—*Sales manager.* This is one who earns a living motivating people to do things which, left to the people to decide, they wouldn't ordinarily do.

No, this is not a mistake. The same definition applies to both salesperson and sales manager. The difference between the two jobs lies in the different interpretations of the job descriptions.

A salesperson's job is to motivate people (in this case, customers) to do something (purchase) that they wouldn't ordinarily do, while a sales manager's job is to motivate people (in this case, salespeople) to do something (sell) that they wouldn't ordinarily do.

Salespeople become successful by motivating customers to make decisions on matters they wouldn't have ordinarily even considered. That's why they're called salespeople, because they sell. Yet, salespeople also become successful by being motivated to sell, because, many times, salespeople would do virtually nothing without proper direction. This is where the sales manager comes into play.

A competent sales manager must be able to motivate the sales force not only to sell, but to sell more by getting increased orders, making more contacts and developing new customers.

Of course, if that were the only job of a sales manager, life would be a breeze, wouldn't it? But that's just one small part of a competent sales manager's responsibilities. In fact, the next chapter would be appropriate to identify the five jobs of a manager, along with the eight most common problems most sales managers face that eventually do them in. Stick with me into the next chapter to learn how to make the most of your positions.

IN A CAPSULE

1. Sales managers can enjoy their work immensely and be successful at the same time by making their salespeople's jobs as much fun as possible. Managers who maintain solemn business atmospheres usually work harder, have more headaches and get fewer rewards because no one is having fun.

2. Every successful sales organization rests upon a solid, three-point foundation consisting of a sound business plan, the right people and strong leadership. If any point of the triangle is weak, the sales organization will be weak accordingly.

3. Successful sales organizations operate under sound organizational charts that link each salesperson to only one supervisor. To make a salesperson (or sales manager) responsible and accountable to more than one person can lead to costly frustration.

4. The job descriptions of sales manager and salesperson is the same; they're both people who earn a living motivating people to do things which, left to the people to decide, they wouldn't ordinarily do. Salespeople motivate customers, and sales managers motivate salespeople.

List the most important points you have gained from the
preceding Strategy:

_____

_____

_____

_____

_____

_____

_____

_____

_____

_____

_____

_____

_____

_____

_____

_____

_____

_____

Strategy 2:

Patch the Cracks

Suppose you were hired to manage a team of salespeople for a business that had yet to open its doors. In fact, the team of salespeople you were charged to manage was, at the time of your hiring, non-existent. Unless someone were willing to do the job for you, you would have to recruit the sales team. Then you would have to train them to operate in accordance with company policy, direct them as to their particular areas of responsibility, motivate them to get the job done and, when necessary, upgrade the operation.

In short, the five jobs of a sales manager are to **recruit, train, direct, motivate** and **upgrade.** It might even sound like the same responsibilities that any manager of any organization might have, but for one major difference—the nature of the business and the people who are hired to sell.

As I said in the introduction, managing salespeople is different from managing salaried employees. To illustrate my point, I was hired by the "Big Boy" restaurant chain in Michigan to stage a seminar for franchise owners in 1982, a time when the economy of Michigan was, to say the least, decidedly depressed. The economy was so bad that many Michigan residents sought jobs in the oil fields of Texas and Louisiana, where scores of automobile bumper stickers read, "Would the last person to leave Michigan please turn out the lights?" And in Michigan at that time, the home of U.S. automakers, a different bumper sticker was popular: "Hungry? Eat your Toyota!"

Yet, I found at this seminar that it was quite difficult to uncover potential problems to discuss with these franchise owners. Since the economy was bad, they were having little if any problem hiring and retaining employees to cook, operate cash registers, wait tables and clean the buildings—at minimum wage—because people would virtually cut backflips on command to keep their jobs.

However, during those bleak economic times, a manager of salespeople faced an entirely different situation altogether. When the economy is bad, salespeople very badly need day-to-day direction and motivation. Salespeople are often self-starters. When the economy is good, they usually can start with little or no trouble. But when the economy is bad, a sales manager's motivating and directing skills will be needed, because salespeople will find it harder to get started.

WATCH YOUR STEP!

Even when a sales manager is competent in each of the five areas of expertise, problems may be encountered if he or she should step into a crack in the foundation.

A crack in the business foundation is a flaw that, left to exist, will eventually topple a sales organization and, in the meantime, will frustrate any sincere efforts to boost production.

There are eight common cracks in sales organizations' foundations. Be aware of them, and you'll make your job—and your life—much easier and much more fun.

COMMON CRACK NO. 1

Over-extended sales manager

If you are a sales manager who, in addition to your regular full-time duties, also oversees the organization (also a full-time job) plus serves as the company's top sales producer (another full-time job), your family eventually may forget what you look like. But tell them to take heart; you'll be home soon, because your company either will fold or you'll burn out to the point of inefficiency and be replaced by another workhorse.

Again, a sales manager's job is to **recruit, train, direct, motivate** and **upgrade** the team of sales associates. That should be the manager's only job. An over-extended manager is serving neither his or her own best interests nor those of the company. Any sales manager who willingly accepts such a situation either is not working for a very good company or is, in effect, saying "I don't trust anybody but me." That's why this manager tries to balance the weight of the world upon his or her shoulders.

This type of thinking must be changed before the manager—and company—can reach full potential.

COMMON CRACK NO. 2

Half of a job description

The number one reason why managers resign, or why they aren't productive, is because they are given the responsibility for **recruiting,**

training, directing, motivating and **upgrading** the sales team, but they are not given the authority to carry out those responsibilities.

For example, suppose a company owner said the following to a sales manager: "Your job is to increase production thirty-six percent, add more staff and rearrange our logistics within our organization so we'll be more effective. But if you need anything, check with me first. And I'll still do the hiring and the firing."

What the owner is saying to the manager is, "I want you to do the job, but I'm not going to give you the authority." A manager can't recruit if he or she can't hire, and a manager certainly cannot upgrade if he or she can't fire. A manager who is given responsibility without authority will never reach his or her full potential. Eventually, the manager will be frustrated right out of the sales business or into the open arms of a competitor who is willing to relinquish the reins of authority in favor of building a top-notch sales force.

COMMON CRACK NO. 3

Trying to pull the organization up from the top

Many managers spend too much time trying to pull salespeople's productions up to a level with the top producer. Instead, they should be continually replacing their worst producers.

For example, Manager A has ten commissioned salespeople, and the top producer is earning $100,000 per year. Manager B also has ten commissioned salespeople. The best isn't making $100,000, but the worst is making $35,000 per year. Who has the better sales force? My guess is Manager B.

In a sales organization, it is imperative to build from the bottom. Who cares if the top producer is earning a hundred grand per year if the other nine members of the team are drawing poverty-level incomes? And who cares what the top producer is making if the worst producer is earning $35,000?

Regardless of whether your team is commissioned or noncommissioned, if your worst producers are continually getting better and better because you're replacing them with better and better people, then the organization can't help but grow as a result.

COMMON CRACK NO. 4

Inconsistent Management

A start-and-stop manager will not be respected by his or her sales team. This is the type of manager who will announce the formation of a new company policy or practice, only to forget about it soon after it is instituted. A manager who never follows through will create a "ho-hum" attitude with the team. The salespeople won't take the manager seriously.

COMMON CRACK NO. 5

Managing the minimum

A weak manager focuses on the top producer; everything he or she does will be designed to satisfy (or pacify) the number one salesperson. The rest of the manager's time will be spent trying to motivate and raise the production of the bottom producer. Consequently, in the case of a ten-member force, this manager will neglect the remaining eighty percent.

The majority of your staff needs your direction and attention. The top producer usually can generate sales without very much, if any, assistance; the bottom producer generally· won't improve no matter what you do.

Also, a manager should manage the maximum to keep turnover low. Most turnover in sales organizations comes from the middle-line producers. The top producer is going to stay on the job until he or she can strike a better deal with another organization; the bottom producer will stay until you throw him or her out the door.

Good managers will concentrate efforts on the majority of the sales force—those whose average, but solid, contributions help make the company what it is.

COMMON CRACK NO. 6

Partnerships

Partnerships generally are not bad if the partners involved learn to do two things—play their personalities and divide authorities and responsibilities.

That means that one should act as administrator (preferably the one who can keep a neat desk) and the other should act as sales manager (more than likely, the one with the cluttered desk). If they disagree on a particular point, they can argue to their heart's content behind closed doors, but they should arrive at a mutual decision and announce it to the staff. Otherwise, the staff is going to be demoralized at the concept of having conflicting chiefs.

COMMON CRACK NO. 7

Managing individuals

Every sales office has a conglomeration of individual personalities. There's Ron the Rebel, the top producer who prides himself on his unwillingness to conform to company standards; Know-It-All Nellie, whose production is above average, but is quick to get in the last word to any directive; Old-Time Otto, who definitely is in the bottom third of producers and is in the sales business only because his doctor told him to take it easy for a while; Walt the Workhorse, who took nineteen orders but will have to spend six months cleaning up his mess; Procrastinating Paula, who needs no additional explanation; Tom the Time-Stealer, who never wants to do anything alone, including work; Nice Neal, who is so nice that he thinks selling is potentially offensive and in poor taste; and Negative Ned, who always looks—and comments, unfortunately—from the darker point of view.

How in the world could you manage a bunch of varied, contrasting individuals such as these? You don't. There's no way you could suit all of them. Your job is to manage the team, and this is done not only by setting rigid company standards, but by adhering to them, too.

COMMON CRACK NO. 8

Low or no standards

I'm not talking about everybody looking nice. I'm talking about high company standards in terms of market projections and personal training. Yet, I've heard some managers say, "My people would not live up to my standards, so I lowered them."

That's not the way to attract quality people to your organization. Take the United States Marines Corps, which has never had a recruiting problem. Despite the fact that the Marines' basic training is second to none in intensity and the fact that Marines usually are the first U.S. service people to become involved in combat, and, consequently, the first to die, there still is a long line of people waiting to get in.

High standards will increase production, not lower it. People always live up to at least the minimum requirements of the law or their company policy. If you have team members who would challenge you on this, perhaps you need to upgrade your staff accordingly with new members who are willing to abide by the company plan.

There are only two ways to attract good people from your competitors to your organization. One is by giving away the farm, which will infuriate other members of your team; the other is by setting high standards and hiring enthusiastic, though inexperienced, salespeople to work the company plan. And when the company has made a name for itself and is known as the company with the highest possible standards, watch the qualified people line up for jobs. The higher the standards, the longer the line waiting to get in.

THE MARK OF A LEADER

You were hired to be a leader, the driving force behind your sales team. So what is leadership? It's the ability to channel individuals toward accomplishing the common objectives, which is the company goal or plan.

Who makes the best leaders? There are three important requirements for a leader. They should have the desire to lead, which is really more important than having the technical management skills; the energy to lead, and it does take energy to manage; and an orientation to people, which is essential in any business involving interaction with people.

A leader should know what motivates salespeople to succeed. Is it money? Yes, but money isn't among the top three motivators; if it were, salespeople wouldn't need sales managers. Is it future opportunity, such as the promise of great things on the horizon for continued hard work and perseverance? If anything, future opportunity demotivates people, because they want their rewards now. Is it better working conditions, such as remodeled offices and better furnishings? That can't hurt, but it won't make or break a sales team.

Do you know that it's much cheaper to retain a good salesperson than it is to recruit a new one? If you want to minimize your turnover, you must give eighty percent of your sales force what it wants, every day.

And there's good news—you can afford this. A national study shows that the three major motivators of salespeople are recognition, participation and sympathetic help.

These three motivators won't cost your company a cent, other than what it takes to compensate you for your time. Salespeople want to be recognized for their performances. That's the number one motivator.

Number two is participation. They want to be a part of the action, to participate in finding solutions to problems. And they must be given an active role in this. To simply ask your salespeople at the end of a business meeting if any of them have anything to contribute to the good of the group isn't enough.

And finally, salespeople want sympathetic help. They want to be told what to do in respectful, helpful terms. They don't want to be corrected in belittling fashion or ridiculed publicly (or privately, for that matter) for not knowing a proper procedure.

Give them recognition, allow them to participate and offer them sympathetic help when needed. In return, they'll give you their all and, simultaneously, you'll get a sales team you'll be quite proud to lead. And it will be the beginning of establishing the right foundation for future success.

So now that you're familiar with a successful sales organization's foundation and the problems that can undermine it, as well as the five jobs of a competent sales manager, let's go on to the next chapter. There, we'll take a look at the job of recruiting—the task that involves getting the right people to build the solid foundation that your organization must have to flourish.

IN A CAPSULE

1. Managing salespeople is different from managing employees of other professions. When economic times are good, salespeople have no trouble motivating themselves to work, because they generally are self-starters. Yet, employees of other professions during good times tend to be lax in their jobs, because the chances of getting other jobs are good. But during bleak economic times, while other employees will work fervently to hang onto their jobs, salespeople very badly need day-to-day direction.

2. The five jobs of a sales manager are to **recruit, train, direct, motivate** and **upgrade.** If a sales manager attempts to take on other responsibilities, he or she might become overextended and, as a result, potentially ineffective.

3. Sales managers who are given responsibility without authority also will eventually be frustrated out of the business or will head for the competition.

4. Successful sales managers build their sales organizations from the bottom. They replace low producers with better producers. Consequently, they have better organizations than those managers who are more concerned with their top producers.

5. Start-and-stop sales managers usually aren't respected by their salespeople. Successful sales managers are consistent; they don't announce plans unless they intend to follow through with them.

6. Sales managers who devote too much attention to their top and bottom producers are committing the sin of ignoring the majority of their sales forces. Successful sales

managers manage the maximum, which contributes the majority of sales to the organization.

7. Partnerships can be fine if both partners iron out problems in private and announce mutually agreeable decisions. Otherwise, salespeople will be demoralized at conflicting directives and decisions.

8. Successful sales managers manage teams, not individuals, by setting rigid company standards and demanding that they be followed by all.

9. Successful sales managers attract and keep good salespeople with high standards.

10. Sales managers can become good leaders by giving salespeople what they need. The three best motivators of salespeople are recognition, participation and sympathetic help.

List the most important points you have gained from the
preceding Strategy:

_____

_____

_____

_____

_____

_____

_____

_____

_____

_____

_____

_____

_____

_____

_____

_____

_____

NOTES

Section 2

RECRUITING

Strategy 3:

Recruiting—Begin at the Beginning

Let's set the stage for a success scenario: You're the manager of a ten-member sales team, which recently broke the company record for monthly sales. The owner is happy with you and you're happy with your team. Everything is sailing smoothly, and you're sitting on top of the world with ten competent and able salespeople holding you up.

Building this team was no easy effort. It took months upon months of directing, training and motivating the slow producers to raise their productions, and you've succeeded. Those who didn't respond to your challenge to improve had to be eliminated, and you had to bear the bad news. No matter how much fun you have with your job, you know that firing is one part that is no fun at all.

So you've earned the right to bask in the corporate limelight, which feels awfully good at this point, because you know you had to suffer in the darkness long enough to get there.

You start to relax; after all, your sales team is very competent and able. Their combined efforts last month proved that not only to you, but to the owner. So what could go wrong?

Plenty.

For example, your top salesperson resigns, having landed a better deal with the competition. Your number three producer also leaves to follow a spouse who was given a lucrative promotion involving an out-of-state transfer. Another good producer develops serious health problems and is forced to take early retirement. And still another quits the sales business for good, thanks to an unexpected, but fatal, heart attack.

All of a sudden, your sales team is down by forty percent, and guess who is responsible for filling the vacancies.

That's right. You are.

That means that you've got to get to work and find four good people to replace those that you lost. That's not going to be easy. Furthermore, you know that the chances of setting another company record is slim indeed with a sales team that is forty percent novice.

All of a sudden, somebody just switched off the corporate lime-light and pushed you off the top of the world.

Don't you just hate it when your top producers leave? It means you have to look elsewhere for others to fill the voids, and you know right away that you'll have trouble finding someone who will be able to work as efficiently and effectively as his or her predecessors.

Many sales managers I know have trouble accepting turnover within their organizations. It's not so much that they begrudge the salespeople for leaving; they just resent having to recruit to fill the vacancies.

Recruiting is a tough job; the recruiter must attract and hire new people who will be competent and able to make worthwhile contributions to the company. Yet the manager knows all too well that the new recruits may prove to be even worse than the all-time worst producers the company has ever employed. The prospect of making company history by being the manager to hire a salesperson who gives an altogether new definition to the word "inept" is always on the manager's mind.

As I pointed out in Chapter One, the five jobs of a manager are to **recruit, train, motivate, direct** and **upgrade.** A successful sales manager must be strong in each of these five jobs, and notice that recruiting comes first.

If you can't recruit, you can't manage people. For starters, you eventually, through attrition, will have no people to manage. On a more serious note, it would be unrealistic to think that you could serve well as a manager by fulfilling satisfactorily the other four duties and leaving recruiting to the business owner.

If you can't develop the basic skills of recruiting—that is, to select personally the people whom you would manage—then why is it realistic to think that you can develop other managerial skills?

A manager who would manage, yet leave recruiting to another, is somewhat comparable to a fisherman who is averse to handling worms. It may not be the most pleasant portion of the job, but it is necessary if the fisher would fish.

A manager who would manage must recruit his or her own salespeople. Remember, managers have five jobs, and they have no more overall effectiveness than they enjoy in the job with which they experience the most difficulty.

Or, to put it in simpler terms, the five jobs are proverbial links in a chain, which is no stronger than its weakest link.

REASONS TO RECRUIT

To develop better skills at recruiting, it's first important to understand why recruiting is necessary. Of course it would appear to even the novice manager that recruiting is necessary to fill vacancies as they arise. But if you wait until then to start your recruiting efforts, you might be waiting too long. Let's look at the five most popular reasons for recruiting:

1. **To build a staff.** If the manager is responsible for opening a new office, he or she will find it necessary to hire a complete team of salespeople. This will require a mass recruiting effort.

2. **To expand a staff.** If your sales team has broken all kinds of records, the company owner may decide to expand operations. To grab a larger share of the market-place, it will be necessary to hire several additional sales-people.

3. **To replace low producers.** Out of every ten salespeople in a typical organization, there is one at the bottom who is never going to succeed, no matter how much training, direction and motivation you offer. It doesn't matter how many chances you give this salesperson, success in sales just isn't in the cards. This person must be replaced, if for no other reason than because he or she is consuming too much of your time, compared to the precious few sales he or she generates. Even the Bible can be used as an effective management manual. It says something to this effect: "Seek not the living among the dead." I've known some managers to say, "Well, the foot-dragger isn't costing me." But there is overhead to consider, and a negative non-producer is taking up desk space without generating the minimum of income your company requires. And for every non-producer who isn't willing to work, there are several good salespeople on the outside just crying for a chance to get in.

4. **To eliminate complacency.** When your sales team is
   working well, leave it alone. But for a paradox, if you
   leave it alone long enough, the team will start to stagnate.
   Then you're going to have to do something to stir up
   the still waters. You can scream and berate, which
   amounts to tossing a boulder into a goldfish pond. Or
   you can, in effect, toss in small pebbles by bringing in
   two or three brand new, enthusiastic salespeople. By
   doing this, the rest of the team is going to be motivated
   into action, so they won't look bad, by comparison.

   To illustrate the effect that new, enthusiastic salespeople may have on an existing team, consider the following: Scientists say that it's physically impossible for
   the bumblebee to fly because of its short wing span
   compared to the weight of its body. But the bumblebee
   doesn't subscribe to the laws of science, so it flies anyway.

   New salespeople are like bumblebees. They often
   don't know that it's impossible to sell certain products
   to particular prospects, so they do it anyway. They're
   great for shaking up the status quo.

5. **To replace normal turnover in the organization.** Your
   children will grow up someday and leave home, and
   your best salespeople will leave you, too. Both are facts
   of life. No matter how strong a team you feel you have
   built, circumstances will always arise that will result
   in your best people leaving you, and the worst time to
   recruit is after you've already lost someone.

I once managed a real estate firm consisting of eight salespeople,
and business had never been better. My salespeople's attitudes and
morale were at all-time highs. But all good things must come to an
end, and suddenly, attitudes and morale started to plunge. I did

some investigating and found out why: One of my salespeople was going into business for himself, and he had four others going with him.

I'm no mathematical genius, but it didn't take a wizard to realize that sixty-two and one-half percent of my sales force was on its way out the door. I had to straighten out the situation by firing the would-be entrepreneur and reassessing the job situations of the other four, two of whom I also discharged. The other two and I reached mutual agreements allowing them to stay on.

Still, my sales force was down by almost forty percent, and I had some recruiting to do. And that is no time to find out that you have to know how to recruit.

Recruiting in some form or another should be an ongoing process to guard against those unexpected, but certain, pitfalls that life in the manager's seat seems to provide. And the manager who understands the importance of the five reasons for recruiting will likely be the manager who realizes the importance of recruiting and will not take that responsibility lightly.

HOW TO RECRUIT

For all things, there is a process, and recruiting is no exception. In fact, I'm going to offer you the best process of recruiting of which I'm aware. I can personally tell you that it has worked well throughout my years of recruiting experience, not just for me, but also for the hundreds of sales managers I've taught to use this system. And if you follow it, I believe you'll agree.

STEP ONE—SET A GOAL.

How many people do you need, what kind of people are you seeking and how soon do you need them? Answer those three questions and you've taken the first step to recruiting. Sales managers often tell new salespeople to establish attainable, written-down goals in their pursuit of success. Yet, these same sales managers often don't stop to realize that the same concept is applicable to their successes as well. After analyzing your situation, if you can determine that you need six full-time salespeople within sixty days, part of your job already is done.

STEP TWO—PROSPECT FOR INTERVIEWS.

This is one of the most misunderstood steps of the recruiting process. Some managers confuse the step of prospecting with the step of selection, and this is indeed a mistake. To prospect simply means to make contact with people who are thinking about changing careers in the not-too-distant future. When these people are located, the manager simply completes the prospecting phase by scheduling a bona fide interview with them. That's all.

STEP THREE—STAGE THE FIRST INTERVIEW.

The interview should be a face-to-face, one-on-one session between prospect and manager. This is simply a session with the prospect to get a few facts and a first impression as to whether you would like to work with him or her. But by all means, don't even think of attempting to hire a person on the first interview. This is the worst thing you could do. I realize that, sometimes, hiring someone outright might be tempting, but most of the time, you're going to be setting yourself up for a fall.

If you ask someone to make a decision on coming to work for

you on the basis of a forty-five minute (or even a two-hour) interview, you're actually asking for more than he or she can deliver. In effect, you'll almost be forcing that person to accept your offer, which increases the chances of your being disappointed later. Either the salesperson's production won't meet your expectations, or the salesperson will break his or her promise to you by accepting a better offer. And worse than not recruiting is the letdown that comes when a person who you think is coming to work for you never shows.

The first interview is only to gather information on the prospect and to convince him or her of the benefits that a sales career has to offer.

STEP FOUR—STAGE A SECOND INTERVIEW.

This is when you make the final selection—after you've had time to review and digest the information you gathered on the first. Remember that the prospect has had time to consider whether he or she wants to work for you, too. That's why it's important to stage the second interview—to give both you and the prospect time to make a decision. You want a firm commitment from the prospect on whether or not to come aboard the proverbial ship, and the second interview is the logical time for this.

And when you ask for the commitment, don't accept an "I want to think it over." There was time to do that after the first interview; the prospect obviously still has at least one objection if he or she can't decide. Get a firm commitment, even if it's a rejection.

STEP FIVE—FOLLOW UP.

In situations where outside training may be necessary before commencing employment, it's important to stay in touch with the prospect to keep him or her interested in your company and its activities.

There! It's as simple as that. Or is it? Well, actually, it's simple to understand, but it's not necessarily easy to follow. Like anything that's worth mastering, this process requires practice. These five steps were capsulized to give you an overview of the basic process of recruiting. We'll explore each step in detail in later chapters.

So after you set your goal, you'll be ready to prospect. You'll have to attract far more prospects than you have positions to fill for two reasons: One—every prospect won't be interested in your organization, and, two—not all of those who are interested will make the grade of joining your team.

So if you would have a steady pool of prospects from which to choose, the process of prospecting is going to involve more than simply contacting one or two people per week. The fewer prospects with whom you touch base, the fewer the qualified and willing applicants you will reach.

Obviously, I really don't have to try too hard to convince you of the importance of prospecting, because you know that through your own personal sales experience. But the process of prospecting for salespeople varies somewhat from the process of prospecting for buyers.

And if you'll follow me into the next chapter, I'll detail a prospecting process for you that helped elevate me to the position (which often has been ascribed to me) as the country's number one results-oriented real estate sales speaker, trainer and consultant.

Again, remember that the process is generic. It won't work any better for a real estate sales manager than it will for sales managers of automobile dealerships, insurance agencies or widget works. No matter what your salespeople sell, if you choose to subscribe to this process, I think you'll find that it will serve you well, too.

IN A CAPSULE

1. If a manager can't recruit, he or she will not be able to manage. If you can't select the people you would manage, you won't be able to develop other necessary managerial skills. The five jobs of a sales manager are proverbial links in a chain, and managers will enjoy no more overall effectiveness than they have in the job that causes them the most difficulty.

2. There are five reasons to recruit new salespeople. Those reasons are to build a staff, to expand a staff, to replace low producers, to eliminate complacency and to replace normal turnover in the organization.

3. There are five steps to successful recruiting. A manager must first set a goal, then prospect for new salespeople. Initial interviews should be staged with prospects, and a second interview should be staged with prospects with potential. After getting a positive commitment from prospects willing to join the organization, the manager must follow up with new employees in cases where outside training may be necessary before actual employment.

List the most important points you have gained from the
preceding Strategy:

_____

_____

_____

_____

_____

_____

_____

_____

_____

_____

_____

_____

_____

_____

_____

_____

Strategy 4:

Find the Right People

$\mathbf{B}$ack in the late 1840's, many Americans would have been singing "California, Here I Come," except for the fact that the song wouldn't be composed until the next century.

Those were the days of the Gold Rush that took the young nation by storm. Many families followed the sun across the United States to find their fortunes, lured by the promise of pay dirt that was waiting for takers.

Of course, not everyone who traveled to the west coast was successful in the search for security. There just wasn't enough gold to go around; only those who were quick to act, willing to work and determined to succeed were rewarded for their efforts.

Those are the same qualities you seek in salespeople you would attract and employ, because you know very well that selling requires work.

After all, gold sought by the ambitious Americans of the 1800's wasn't gift-wrapped and waiting for them. First, they had to travel hundreds upon hundreds of painfully slow miles before even getting the opportunity to comb through California creekbeds. Those who really wanted wealth had to be willing to wade through waters and sift through a great deal of worthless sand before laying claim to the precious ore.

This was the process of prospecting. And as a sales manager, your situation is analogous to those of the old-time prospectors. You see, you want gold, too, (just like virtually everyone). But the Gold Rush was over long before your life (not to mention your career in sales) ever began. So instead of traveling to the west coast with high hopes and a "prospecting pan," it was necessary to find another line of endeavor. So you chose sales, because that's where today's "gold" is.

Now you're a sales manager, and you get your "gold" from the production of your sales team. And to maximize your income, it is essential to recruit and enlist top-notch salespeople who likewise want to maximize their incomes.

Unfortunately, finding such people isn't easy. Like prospectors of old, you have to sift through a lot of sand, so to speak. To find the really talented and dedicated salespeople, you've got to meet a lot of people whom you'll eventually find just won't make the grade.

But if you want the "gold," you must be willing to prospect. And I want to share with you my process of prospecting that put "gold" into my pockets and, if you follow it, will do the same for you.

MAKE CONTACTS

What exactly do we mean by "prospecting?" Simply stated, prospecting is making contact with people thinking about starting, or changing, their careers in the not-too-distant future. That's all.

It is not necessary that they be considering a career in sales; it will be your job later to acquaint them with the benefits of the profession. During the prospecting phase, you simply want to concern yourself with people who are interested in starting a new career.

Why not prospect for people who already have satisfying careers? After all, might they not make good salespeople? Of course they could. But a person who is satisfied with his or her current career generally enjoys sufficient compensation and is creatively challenged by the demands of the profession. As a rule, it will be difficult to offer such a person an attractive alternative to his or her current career.

However, studies show that a majority of North Americans are unhappy with their careers, and many of them utterly detest their jobs. The reason for this undoubtedly is because the compensation is insufficient and/or the job itself is not sufficiently challenging.

That's most unfortunate for the majority of North Americans. But that's very fortunate for you, because your prospecting pool is bountiful, indeed. So start making contact with these people. They won't be hard to find.

And how do you prospect? Any way you'd like. If you like to approach people in supermarkets or on the street to ask them if they're considering career changes, do it. That's a good form of prospecting. In fact, any way you want to prospect is a good way.

When prospecting, you've got to take the attitude of young Michael O' Reilly, a member of a small New England parish. Being the good Catholic that he was, he never hesitated to go to confession whenever he felt he had sinned.

"Bless me, Father, for I have sinned," Michael said. "I have committed hanky-panky."

The priest wanted to grant Michael absolution, but first, it was necessary for Michael to confess his sins in detail.

"Who was the girl?" the priest asked. "Was it Mary at the bakery?" Michael shook his head. "Was it Susie at the library?" the priest persisted. "No, father, not her. Please don't ask me to tell you; I can't."

"Okay," the priest sighed. "But I want you to come back next week."

On his way down the steps to the church, Michael met a friend who knew the reason why Michael was there.

"Hey, Michael," the friend called. "Did the priest grant you absolution?"

"No," Michael replied. "But I got a week off and two good leads."

Of course I would never suggest that you do anything wrong to get a lead. But the fact is, there is no wrong or bad way to find prospects; any way you can find them is good. But there are better ways and, ultimately, the best way is one which brings you the greatest number of qualified people. And, generally, the best way usually requires the greatest effort.

As a sales manager, don't spend your time with the easiest methods of prospecting; go for the methods that offer the best results.

GOOD PROSPECTING METHODS

For your information, I'd like to review with you some good methods of prospecting, though they're not necessarily the best. I'm listing these not so much because I want you to subscribe to them for recruiting efforts, but because they may be valuable to you for other reasons, which I will explain.

1. **Pay bounties to salespeople.** You possibly can recruit new salespeople by offering financial rewards to your existing sales team members who can bring prospects to you. But remember, money doesn't motivate salespeople as much as recognition, participation and sympathetic help. And also, if your existing sales team members

are weak, chances are good they'll bring in weak recruits.

If you do offer bounties, cover yourself by making two things clear to your sales team. One, the first part of the bounty will be paid only when the recruit is hired and the remainder will be paid only after the new employee passes a probationary period. Two, the bounty system does not give the salesperson the privilege of offering employment to their friends; reserve the responsibility of hiring for yourself, as you should, of course.

2. **Establish a booth at a trade show or county fair.** Many sales managers expend great efforts to establish recruiting booths at mass gatherings. This actually is great for public relations for your company; in terms of recruiting, a booth may attract a couple of bona fide prospects.

3. **Career nights.** Many managers believe that an advertisement for such an event staged at a local hotel will attract a swarm of prospects. I've been involved in no less than three hundred career nights, and I feel qualified to say that this just isn't the case. Career nights are terrific forums to convince prospects to join your team, to remotivate your existing salespeople and to boost your company's image in the marketplace. But in terms of actually attracting prospects, it offers low returns.

If you stage a career night, make sure that all of your salespeople are required to show up with their company identification tags and at least one guest. Otherwise, you'll be lucky to wind up with more than just a few warm bodies. And a poorly attended career night is worse than no career night at all from the standpoint of company image.

Make sure the location of the event is easily accessible to the public. Station an existing salesperson at each table to chat with prospects. You may or may not be the right person to conduct the session. Career nights should be mini-motivational and informational seminars with three themes—the benefits of a sales career, the benefits of working with your company and a motivational period during which the leader describes the success that can be attained in the sales profession. If a prospect shows considerable interest in a sales career, don't hire the prospect right away; merely set a mutually agreeable time for a first interview. Career night should be a prospecting tool, not a group selection or hiring method.

4. **Circulate brochures.** Brochures are great for helping to convince the prospect to participate in a career interview. But as recruiting tools, they simply don't work.

A better method of recruiting is to use your own salespeople, just like with the bounty system. Surprisingly, you get better results when you don't offer bounties. When you enlist your salespeople's assistance by stressing the benefits of recruiting that they and the company will derive, you get them participating in the company cause. Remember: In most cases, the opportunity to participate is a stronger motivator than money.

Also, salespeople will be more conscientious in their searches for recruits if they are not financially rewarded. Under the bounty system, the monetary reward might entice a salesperson to bring in anyone he or she can convince, cajole or coerce into applying for a position.

But consider the effect on your salespeople if you tell them the following: "Gang, I'm going to ask you to do something for me that I think will help us all grow faster in the marketplace. We're expanding, and we need some more salespeople. But it's very important to me that we get the right kind of people, and since like attracts like, I need your help in finding several good salespeople like yourselves."

A little praise goes a long way. To be sure that they don't disappoint you (or disgrace themselves in your eyes), your salespeople will be particularly careful in their searches for the right types of prospects.

A CHAIN OF EVENTS

Prospecting is a chain of events that begins when you meet the prospect. At that point, all you should want to do is schedule the first interview. Don't discuss income or other factors until later. If the prospect asks about it, tell him or her the topic can be discussed during the interview.

Many sales managers are their own worst enemies. They look around for prospects, only to scare them away when they find them by discussing compensation or other phases of the business. So don't attempt during the initial meeting—whether it's at a cocktail party or a career night—to persuade the prospect to get involved in the sales business. To start selling then would be "overkill." You'll have plenty of time for "selling" the sales business later, during the interview.

All you want to do during the initial contact is to persuade the prospect to participate in a career interview. But there are two important things I want you to do when prospecting:

1. **Project selectivity.** Don't give your prospect the feeling that you're willing to interview anyone who will sit still. Project selectivity by saying something to the effect of, "Maybe sales just isn't for you, so before we set an appointment, let me just ask you a few questions." Then proceed to step two.

2. **Prequalify the prospect.** You'll save a great deal of valuable interview time by finding out whether the pros-

pect shows an interest in undertaking a sales career. You can determine this by asking a few probing questions to determine whether the prospect has sales aptitude and interest. Just as a salesperson prequalifies to separate suspects from prospects and lookers from buyers, a good sales manager will prequalify to separate bona fide candidates from non-candidates.

If you take these steps, you'll attract better candidates, plus you'll have fewer "no-shows" for your interviews.

But I suppose I've kept you in suspense long enough. You want to learn the best way of prospecting, and I don't blame you. So I'm going to give you the best recruiting method I know. But brace yourself. Although it's legal, moral, ethical, honest and won't kill you, it isn't traditional. Nine times out of ten, whenever I mention this method in a seminar or during a consultation, many sales managers will interrupt me by saying, "Hey, wait a minute, we've tried this, and it doesn't work."

It will work, provided you know the right way to follow the process. And the method itself? Classified advertising that projects selectivity and prequalifies prospects for you.

YOU'VE GOT TO WORD IT RIGHT!

If I were with you right now, I could open the classified section of your local newspaper and show you scores of help-wanted sales ads that won't produce results, simply because they aren't correctly worded to attract prospects.

A newspaper's classified section is the best way to reach the greatest number of people in the least amount of time and with the least amount of expense. But an entire page of advertising space won't bring results if the wording of the ad itself doesn't draw the reader's interest.

You won't need a whole page; four or five simple lines will be enough. Since most people are unhappy with their jobs, many of them check the classifieds daily to scout for new opportunities. They will at least scan your ad; if it's worded properly, they'll actually study it.

Let me tell you how good this system is. I know a sales manager in Texas who picked up this idea at one of my seminars and put it to use. During the next seminar I staged in his area, he approached me during a break.

"Floyd, you S.O.B.," he said, opting instead for the unabbreviated version. I thought he was mad at me, and I didn't want that, because he was a living example of how everything grows big in Texas.

"What's wrong?" I asked.

"That darned (he didn't really say "darned") recruiting method you taught me works! I hired seven people within two weeks with it, and I had never been able to do that before."

Then there was the sales manager in another part of the country who purchased ad space in his local newspaper, used my system, then took off for a two-day vacation. When he returned, his secretary informed him that he had received seventy callers inquiring about the opportunity.

In fact, I could list for you the names of more than thirty sales organization managers and owners who got into the business on this very same ad that I'm about to detail. And they continue to use it, because it works for them.

It will work for you, too. Proceed to the next chapter and I'll explain why.

IN A CAPSULE

1. If you want a top-notch sales force, you must be willing to prospect for good salespeople. Like the gold prospectors of old discovered, prospecting is no easy job, but it's the only way to get the "gold."

2. Prospecting basically is just making contact with people who are interested in starting, or changing, their careers in the near future. It's not necessary that the people be considering a sales career. That will be your job to "sell" them on a sales career later.

3. Studies show that most North Americans are at least unhappy with their jobs, and a good portion actually detest them. That means your prospecting pool should be vast, indeed.

4. Any way you want to prospect is good. There is no bad way. Some ways are better than others. Some good ways of prospecting include paying bounties to salespeople, establishing a booth at a county fair, staging career nights and circulating brochures.

5. A better way of prospecting involves simply asking your employees to recommend potential salespeople. Ironically, results will be better, even though your salespeople aren't financially rewarded, because they'll have the opportunity to participate—a strong motivator for salespeople. Since money is not the primary motivator they'll be more conscientious in their searches.

6. When making contact with a prospect, you should project selectivity and prequalify the prospect. Projecting selectiv-

ity gives the prospect the impression that you won't hire just anyone. And prequalifying the prospect will save you some time later by weeding out prospects who have absolutely no interest in a sales career.

List the most important points you have gained from the
preceding Strategy:

_____

_____

_____

_____

_____

_____

_____

_____

_____

_____

_____

_____

_____

_____

_____

_____

_____

Strategy 5:

Write the Right Ad

During the Korean War, there was a concerted effort to interest G.I.'s in a government life insurance policy that would pay their next-of-kin $10,000 in the event of their in-service deaths. Ten grand was quite a chunk of change in the early 1950's (not that it's anything to sneeze at now).

Surprisingly, military officials discovered that there were relatively few takers. They thought it was strange, indeed, that soldiers would not be interested in such a policy, even though they were stationed at a world "hot spot" where the regular exchange of bullets and missiles was quite commonplace. And the strangest part of the mass refusal was the fact that it wasn't the price of the policy that discouraged the soldiers from being insured. Any soldier could have a policy for the mere effort of requesting it. There was absolutely no charge. But to take advantage of the free offer, it was necessary for the soldiers to sign up for it.

For the most part, they weren't doing it. Military officials tried in vain to motivate the G.I.'s to take advantage of the government's free offer. They even tried to shame them into taking out policies, reminding soldiers that their families would very likely need the insurance benefits should the very worst occur.

Still, there were few takers. After all, soldiers (and people in general) don't like to think about dying, especially when they're young. But there was a sergeant of a particular platoon who knew that the proper delivery of the correct message could inspire his troops to sign up. One day, he called the G.I.'s to assembly.

"Men," the sergeant said, "The government is offering you a free life insurance policy that will pay your next-of-kin $10,000 should you die in the line of duty. This means that, at absolutely no cost to you, your wives and families will receive a substantial financial settlement should you be killed. But you must take advantage of this offer by signing up for it. If you don't sign up, and if you should die on the battlefield, your survivors will receive absolutely nothing.

"Now I understand that you fellows don't like to think about dying, so let's look at the practical side of this matter. Some of you will sign up, and some of you won't. The government will pay some survivors $10,000, while some survivors won't get a cent. So my question to you is this: When it's time to select troops to send to the front line, which ones do you think will go first? The insured or uninsured?"

The sergeant didn't say another word. Additional words weren't necessary. He had delivered his message most effectively, and as a result, the entire platoon signed up for free insurance before the day was out.

I don't use this story to bring back bad memories of the grim realities of war. Instead, I offer it to illustrate how people who initially reject a particular message ultimately can be persuaded. In this case, the message persuaded the soldiers because it got their attention, appealed to their interest, stimulated their desire to act and, as a result, motivated them into action.

When you're writing classified ads to attract salespeople, that's exactly what you must do—word it to get the readers' attention, appeal to their interests, stimulate their desires and motivate them into action.

Of course, your approach should be somewhat softer than the one used by the sergeant. You wouldn't threaten potential salespeople with the prospect of being shot for not doing what you want until after you hire them.

All jokes aside, using classified ads is the most effective way to reach the most people with the least effort. However, you must remember that your message will be just one among scores of other similar messages from businesses in your area. If you want to have potential salespeople single out your ad from the masses, it will be your responsibility to get the message right.

SELLING IS SELLING IS SELLING

Whether your company sells real estate, insurance, automobiles, vacuum cleaners, encyclopedias, pots and pans, pet rocks, famous metropolitan bridges or secluded swampland, the process is the same: Certain things must occur in customers' minds before they will be motivated to act. When you're recruiting new salespeople, you're actually selling gainful employment to people who are willing to pay for it with work.

If you've had a sterling career as a salesperson, you might think you could sell two milking machines to a farmer with only one cow, and then take the cow as a down payment. You may have every confidence that you could convince a prospect to take on a career selling whatever it is your company has to offer.

But remember, you'll never get your chance to sell if your ad isn't noticed. So the first thing the ad must do is catch the reader's attention. While scanning through the multitudes of classified ads (as disgruntled employees are wont to do), the first sight of your ad must carry an impact similar to stepping barefooted upon a discarded, burning cigarette—the reader should stop and take notice!

If the reader doesn't stop and take notice when seeing your ad, you've lost a prospect. So one good way to catch readers' attention is not to turn them off with your ad.

MOST ADS TURN OFF

Most classified ads discourage many good potential salespeople for one simple reason—they reveal the type of job being offered.

For example, an ad that starts with ''Salespeople Wanted'' will discourage many people who may not be able to envision themselves in sales, even though they, in reality, may prove to be quite competent as salespeople.

To illustrate my point, whenever I conduct a real estate management seminar, I conduct an impromptu survey of those in attendance. Invariably, I find that sixty to seventy percent of the people present were ushered into the sales profession by a friend, because at the time, they had absolutely zero confidence in themselves as salespeople.

Remember, selling is selling is selling. If a majority of successful real estate sales managers today once were unable to envision themselves as salespeople—let alone as managers—then wouldn't it stand to reason that the same thing applies to salespeople in other fields? Certainly.

So if you begin your ad with any mention of sales, you'll actually discount many good prospects. They'll see your ad and think, ''Hey, I know there's money in sales, but I don't think I have what it takes.''

Now bear in mind that these people don't consciously say that to themselves; the thought process occurs within a split second. When they see the position involves sales, all they consciously note is a big risk. So they move on to the next ad, and you lose.

MAKE YOUR AD A MIRROR

How can you make a classified advertisement a mirror? What do you want to do, have the reader see himself or herself in it? Precisely.

After the reader's attention is sufficiently attracted, you have to keep the reader's curiosity by wording the ad to appeal to his or her interests. Just like the G.I.'s envisioned themselves being the first to go to the front line, you want your reader to see himself or herself gainfully employed.

You do that by describing the job qualifications in simple terms that would appeal to the average reader.

I've seen some classified ads that I thought were geared to Superman or Wonder Woman. For example, "Salespeople wanted. Must have late-model luxury car, no less than five years experience and desire to work difficult, demanding territory. College education preferred."

Who would call on an ad like that? Very few people, because the number of good prospects to contact you will decrease as the list of qualifications increases.

You can make most readers see themselves in your ad by keeping it simple. For example, it might read like this: "Local office of national organization (if applicable) needs X number of people willing to work hard and be trained."

Think for a moment. If a person seeking a new position read the previous sentence in a help-wanted ad, would he or she be turned off? Only if the person wasn't willing to work or be trained. And those are the people you don't want.

Or let's put it another way. Suppose you are looking for several new salespeople, and I called you and said, "Hey, I know a person who wants full-time employment, is willing to be trained and would like to talk with you."

Would you talk with the person? I hope you would, because he or she just might be a budding super salesperson just waiting to be developed.

The only thing you should want to accomplish with the ad is to attract prospects and generate phone calls so you can set interviews. That's all. Trying to accomplish anything else with the ad is a mistake. If your qualifications discourage good people, they won't call, and you lose again.

PROJECT SELECTIVITY

Remember, in the preceding chapter, I promised to show you how to project selectivity in your ad. This is a simple matter of arithmetic and common sense. At the point in your ad where you state that you're looking for X number of people, divide X by two. For example, if you're seeking six salespeople, you should only advertise for three. If you're seeking four, ask for only two. If you need two, advertise for one.

The lower the number of salespeople sought, the greater selectivity you project. Think of the psychological impact on the reader who sees your ad calling for a few salespeople. That indicates to the reader that there are only a few vacancies to fill, which indicates that the position must be somewhat lucrative and interesting.

On the other hand, if you put in your ad that you're interested in hiring as many people as possible, the reader will think, "Hey, anybody and his brother could fit into this organization. It must be a loser.''

Then, they'll go on to the next ad, and you lose again.

MAKE THEM SAY "WOW"

Once the ad has attracted the reader's attention and interest, it should stimulate desire. It should offer something appealing. In the case of the G.I.'s and the sergeant's "sales pitch," the soldiers' strong desire to avoid getting shot motivated them to take action that would help ensure their safety. Once the sergeant's message became clear, the soldiers undoubtedly said "Wow" or something equivalent, if only to themselves.

Your ad should list benefits that will make readers say, "Wow," if only to themselves. Now, of course, you could offer the world on a platter, or "blue sky" your readers. But remember, you want to reach numbers of people, and good qualified people at that.

So keep the benefits general and designed to appeal to the greatest number of people. Phrases such as "earn while you learn," "we will train you" and "choice of locations" will attract more people than a teaser such as "earn $100,000 or more your first year" or, worse yet, "unlimited income." Average readers either won't believe such promises, or they'll become discouraged, because they will believe they aren't capable of earning such high salaries.

Keep compensation promises general and geared to the average person's expectations for the same reason that you shouldn't mention sales in the ad. Although it's true that some commissioned salespeople earn more per year than the company president, those salespeople are few and far between.

Primarily, a good sales manager needs a team of salespeople who each have the desire and ability to earn a medium income each year. That's the type of person you should want to attract. Of course, if they should wind up earning more, then you, the salespeople and the company president can laugh about it all the way to the bank.

GIVE THEM A NUMBER

After you have piqued their interest sufficiently, readers will want to know what step to take next. All that's left is to give them a telephone number to call and the name of a person with whom to speak.

Don't always list your company name. Why? Because it's often hard to conceal the fact your company is a sales organization if you identify it in print.

There is no law that requires you to list your company name, so keep the readers in suspense. Don't try to sell them on a sales career in the ad; you'll do that when you get to speak with them on the telephone.

Make sure that the telephone number listed in the ad is not the main telephone line to the company. If the prospect calls and hears a greeting of "ABC Sales," the receptionist probably will never know why the caller terminated the call without speaking, and you lose again.

Instead, list the number of a private or progressive line to the company so when it rings, you'll know that the caller is a prospect. Then pick up the phone and say, "Hello," instead of "ABC Sales."

So bearing in mind this information, perhaps your ad might read something like this:

"Local office of national organization needs two full-time career-minded individuals willing to work hard and be trained. We offer training. Earn while you learn, choice of locations, potential first-year earnings in excess of $50,000. Call Sam at 555-1212."

A person considering a change in careers would find it difficult not to at least call and find out more about the position. And, of course, that's all you want them to do at this point; you can handle the rest.

FOLLOW THE SCRIPT

The ad itself is designed to attract prospects. But the key to the ad system is the manner in which you handle the incoming calls.

The purpose of the telephone inquiry is to acquaint the sales manager with the caller so the manager can determine whether the caller seems to be a suitable prospect. If the manager likes what he or she hears, an interview can be arranged. If not, the manager can politely terminate the call. (I'll explain how later.)

Prospect cards, or index cards upon which the caller's name and telephone number can be recorded, should be stationed near the telephone. When it rings, you should answer it. If you're not in, your secretary should answer it and take a message only. Don't allow anyone else to talk with prospects; that's your job.

Tone and voice inflection is important. Don't sound like a personnel director; sound like a warm human being. That's the type of person for whom most people would like to work. The caller will form his or her opinion of your organization by the sound of your voice. Keep it pleasant and professional.

After you've picked up the phone and said hello, the caller will say something to the effect that he or she saw your ad and wanted to learn more about it. That's your cue to respond with, "Hey, thanks for calling. By the way, what is your name?"

After the caller gives his or her name, write it down. Then respond by saying, "Before we go further, let me explain the type of job we're offering." Then explain, and conclude by asking, "Does _____ sales sound like something you would be interested in knowing more about?" If the response is "no," you should question it.

Actually, whether the prospect indicates agreement, disagreement or indecision is unimportant, because your response line will be the same in any case: "I think I can convince you that if you're willing to work hard and be trained, you can earn every bit of $50,000 your first year, if not more."

Again, the prospect's answer could vary. He or she might say, "Great!" Or the response might be a sharp "Bull feathers." Either way, your response will be the same.

"I've got an idea. Why don't we get together, get to know each other and talk about the possibility of your joining our organization?"

Then, it's up to the prospect. If the prospect agrees, your mission, for the moment, is accomplished. If the prospect is indecisive or absolutely averse to the sales profession, he or she will let you know. And that's your cue for your response.

"If you had known the position involved sales, would you have called?" On the prospect's cue of "No," you can continue by saying, "That's exactly why we didn't identify the position as involving sales. We've found that more than half of successful salespeople never considered sales until they learned all the facts and were shown that they had the potential for success. They actually went to work for an organization that helped them succeed. And I think I can show you how you, too, can succeed, if you'll give me the opportunity. Could you come by this afternoon, or would tomorrow be better?"

If the prospect is simply not interested or is irate because you didn't list sales in the ad (and this is rare, indeed), then you've done all you can do. Thank the caller for calling, then terminate the call. But if the caller is interested, set an appointment.

Now, to make good an earlier promise, suppose the caller sounds very young, non-professional or otherwise unsuited to a career in sales at this time. You can get rid of the caller by overqualifying him or her over the telephone.

Ask the caller to describe his or her wardrobe. Then ask the caller to describe his or her automobile. Then ask the caller how long he or she could survive without an income. Point out the necessity for several good suits or outfits, the advantages of having a late-model, dependable vehicle and the possibility of surviving on reduced income at first. That should dissuade the caller from asking more questions.

But before you hang up, ask the caller if he or she can give you a sales lead. It can't hurt.

Some of your callers undoubtedly will be headstrong and possibly a little suspicious. Before they'll even give you their names, they'll insist on getting information about the job. Don't give it. If the caller takes control of you over the telephone, just think of what a hard time you'll have controlling the person should he or she be hired.

Only set interviews with those people with whom you think, at least at this point, you would like to employ. If your instincts tell you that the person would be unsuitable for employment, trust your instincts. Don't waste your time with an interview.

So there it is, the best recruiting system I know. The words of the ad and your responses are not so important as the concepts behind them. Subscribe to them to the last detail, and I believe you'll find this recruiting system will attract enough good prospects to keep you busy and your team vacancies filled.

And that's not an idle promise. Let me close this chapter with one last illustration to prove my point: A sales manager in Florida ran this type ad in a local newspaper, but his secretary, who actually delivered the ad copy to the newspaper office, mistakenly submitted as part of the ad the complete transcript of the telephone script I previously detailed.

As a result, the ad ran in the newspaper, followed immediately by "Hello . . . Thanks for calling. By the way, what is your name? . . . Before we go further, let me explain the type of job we're offering. . . . Does a career in sales sound like it appeals to you? . . . I think I can convince you that if you're willing to work hard and be trained, you can make at least $50,000 per year, if not more. . . . I've got an idea. Why don't we get together, get to know each other and talk about the possibility of you joining our organization. . . . If you had known the position involved sales, would you have called? . . . That's exactly why we didn't identify the position as involving sales. We've found that more than half of successful salespeople never considered sales until they learned all the facts and were shown that they had the potential for success. They actually went to work for an organization that helped them succeed. And I think I can show you how you, too, can succeed, if you'll give me the opportunity. Could you come by this afternoon, or would tomorrow be better?''

Quite a blunder, wasn't it? Would you believe this manager still received more than thirty calls in one day?

With this system, you can't lose. You'll have more people to interview than you would get with any other single method of prospecting. So go ahead and place the ad in your local newspaper, then stick with me into the next chapter, where I'll tell you how to conduct the interview with the prospect.

IN A CAPSULE

1. Prospecting classified ads should be worded in a manner to attract readers' attention, appeal to their interests, stimulate their desires and motivate them into action.

2. Classified ads are the most effective way to reach the most people with the least effort. But there is competition in the classified section. If you want to have potential salespeople single out your ad from the masses, it will be your responsibility to get the message right.

3. Don't turn off your reader by describing the position as involving sales. Many good salespeople once thought they weren't suited for sales, until they were encouraged into the business by friends. By identifying the position as involving sales, you'll discourage a lot of good people who may happen to lack confidence in themselves as salespeople.

4. Make readers see themselves in your ad by keeping qualifications simple. The only thing you should want to accomplish with the ad is to attract prospects and generate telephone calls so you can set interviews. That's all.

5. Project selectivity in your ad by asking for half the number of applicants you actually need. If you need to fill four positions, announce that you only need to fill two. The more positions you offer, the more prospects will perceive your company as a loser.

6. Don't "blue sky" readers with promises of grand benefits. They either won't believe it, or they'll assume they're not capable of earning such high salaries. Keep compensation promises general and geared to the average person's

73

expectations to ensure the greatest response from the public.

7. Don't list the company name with the ad, lest you discourage potential applicants who don't see themselves as salespeople. List only a telephone number, and one to a private or progressive line. Answer that phone with "Hello." Again, don't answer with your company name, or the caller may hang up.

8. Follow the ad caller script when answering calls. No matter what the caller says, your response will be the same. The script will show you what to say and when, as well as give you control of the call.

9. If the caller sounds too young or non-professional, you can discourage the caller by overqualifying him or her over the telephone. Point out that an applicant must have several good suits, a good dependable automobile and enough money to survive without income at first.

10. Only set interviews with people with whom you think you would like to employ, based on your conversation with them. If you talk with someone who insists on getting information about the job without giving you a name, forget the caller. If you can't control them over the telephone, you'll never be able to control them at work.

List the most important points you have gained from the
preceding Strategy:

_____

_____

_____

_____

_____

_____

_____

_____

_____

_____

_____

_____

_____

_____

_____

_____

_____

Strategy 6:

Successful Interviewing

After you've talked with your prospect on the telephone, if you like what you hear, then schedule an appointment with the prospect for an interview. This is a significant step, which allows you to spend time thinking about whether the prospect fits your bill, and the prospect has the same question in mind.

Take heart. Interviewing, like recruiting, prospecting, selling and climbing a flight of stairs, is a step-by-step process (pardon the pun.)

There are five steps to successful interviewing, and we'll detail these in this and the next chapter. They are:

1. **Explain why you're hiring.**

2. **Describe the type of person you're looking for.**

3. **Ask interview questions.**

4. **Stage a visual presentation.**

5. **Schedule a second interview.**

The purpose of this chapter is to help you select the most qualified applicant possible and, at the same time, to convince the applicant that your company offers him or her the best chance of success.

Learning how qualified the applicant is depends upon good interviewing skills, which will be detailed in this chapter.

GREET THE APPLICANT

The first thing you should do is greet the applicant. If the applicant is on time, let him or her know that you know. If the applicant is late, let him or her know that you know this, too. And if the applicant is early, let him or her wait. These are control tactics, which are good for helping you understand the applicant.

Then, before any interview actually begins, have the applicant fill out an application designed to give you basic information about the applicant and clues as to what questions to ask.

Nineteen out of twenty applicants will fill out the application without argument. But there occasionally will be one rebel who first will want answers to his or her questions.

Don't give them the answers. If the applicant insists on answers before filling out the application, insist on having the applicant fill out the application first. Stress to the applicant that the application will be confidential. For the most part, you can win over resisters.

But if you do get someone who just won't agree to fill out an application until he or she gets some answers, then I personally recommend that you don't even talk with this applicant. If you have problems with the applicant during the interview phase, just think of how much trouble he or she will cause you later. If someone is willing to buck you before he or she even gets the job, let some other sales manager get the headaches. You don't need them.

APPLICATION—KISS

When devising your application, KISS, or Keep It Simple, Sales manager. I've seen some applications that would take an hour or more to fill out. They're very time consuming, and an applicant's enthusiasm can be lost during such a laborious process.

I use a simple two-page application that covers four different areas—personal information, past employment, education and self-analysis, which involves the applicant stating why he or she is seeking a career in sales. Even though they may have been pointed in your direction by a friend or an advertisement, most applicants will say something positive about sales; for the most part, they won't state, "I wasn't interested until a friend recommended it." Many applicants list, "I like people." That's not necessarily a prerequisite for a sales career, but it doesn't hurt at all.

An applicant also can be asked his or her current financial situation, which is a perfectly legal application question. This should give you a pretty good picture of the stability of the applicant. Most good applicants will simply write one word: good. Your poorer applicants will write poor or average, and your bad apples will spell out the grim details: had a divorce four months ago, a little bit behind because . . . That's a warning signal. Pay attention to it.

The filling out of the application not only gets you preliminary information, but it's also a good control tactic to determine how well the applicant takes direction.

TWENTY QUESTIONS

After the application is completed, don't allow the applicant to sit alone for very long. Bring the applicant into your office or some other private setting and ask the secretary to hold your calls. Then, begin your interview.

How do you start? Do you remember a game called "Twenty Questions," in which someone would think of a person and you had to find out who that person was by asking twenty questions? The same process is involved with interviewing. You have to find out who that person is before you will even consider hiring him or her. The only way you can find out is to ask questions.

So I've prepared a list of twenty questions that will help you determine an applicant's potential value to you. Offer the applicant a cup of coffee and glance over the application, paying particular attention to personal history. If there are any blank areas, ask the questions and fill in the answers yourself.

Then ask the applicant for permission to ask questions and write down the answers. Few, if any, applicants would object; some may ask you to discuss income first, but you can handle that obstacle by politely insisting that you be allowed to ask questions first.

Then you can begin with a short statement, such as, "Our organization has been in the marketplace for a number of years. We want to expand, but we want to be very selective. Before we leave today, I hope to give you enough information so we both can make logical decisions."

Then begin your interview questions. They're listed below:

1. **What other types of jobs have you applied for?** (This will determine whether the applicant has a specialty, if the applicant is unemployed and looking for something to carry them through rough times or if the applicant will take any job he or she can find.)

2. **Why are you leaving your current employment?**
(Most answers are self-explanatory—layoff, company
closes, retirement. But sometimes, you can uncover
potential problems. A very common answer is, "I seem
to work harder than anybody else, but I don't get recognition." That's a warning signal. Chances are good
the situation would remain the same, in the eyes of
the applicant, if he or she came to work for you.)

3. **What are your career objectives?** (If they say, "Making a lot of money," that's a warning signal. Remember,
money doesn't motivate most people. An applicant who
says money is his or her only objective actually is
giving you a warning signal.)

4. **How did you get interested in sales?** (Applicants very
rarely will say, "I wasn't, but you made it sound good
over the phone." Instead, most good applicants will
cite a third person, such as a cousin or uncle already
in sales.)

5. **What do you think it takes to succeed in sales?**
(Some good answers include hard work, honesty, persistence, etc. Any answers that differ significantly from
that vein will warrant closer study.)

6. **What kind of work interests you the most?** (If you
get a point blank answer, such as "Working with people," then expand. Ask the applicant why working
with people is important. This can give you more insight
into the applicant.)

7. **What have you done in the past that shows your initiative or willingness to work?** That you are competitive?
That you want or need money? (Don't ask an applicant
if he or she is willing to work hard, is competitive or
wants money. How do you expect the applicant to

answer? With a "no?" Of course not. Ask the applicant to prove that he or she is a hard worker, is competitive and needs money. Then listen for the answers. If the applicant is already in sales, perhaps the applicant will say, "I'm an independent contractor who works sixty hours per week, fifty-two weeks per year." Or perhaps the applicant is a single parent of five children working full-time and part-time jobs to make ends meet.)

8. **What is your strongest personality trait?** (Make a note of this; it could offer you a very important clue as to why you may or may not wish to hire him or her.)

9. **What is your weakest personality trait?** (If an applicant says, "Need direction often," put that in your file. If you do hire the person and he or she turns out to be non-productive, you can offer direction. If that person should fight you, you have but to refer to the application to illustrate that the person indicated that he or she might need some direction.)

10. **How long do you think you could survive without an income?** (Two to three months is a good answer. If you have an applicant who says, "I don't think I could last a week," consider that to be a warning signal. You might recommend a part-time job to carry them through the licensing and/or training phase.)

11. **How many hours per week are you willing to work?** How many days? How many evenings? Be specific. (This question can tell you a lot. Many homemakers will bring out potential problems, such as, I could work forty hours per week, but evenings are out.)

12. **Where do you see yourself five years from today?** (This will give you an idea as to whether the applicant is goal-oriented.)

13. **Are you involved in a self-improvement program?**
(A "no" answer is not unacceptable, but a "yes" answer carries weight, of course.)

14. **Have you ever been involved in sales training?** (If so, where? This can give you an idea how qualified the prospect may be.)

15. **Are you primarily interested in earning money, or do you think service to your fellow man is satisfactory accomplishment?** (If the answer is service, that's a warning signal. By the same token, if the answer is just money, that's a warning signal, too. But if you get a combination of both, you may have a good applicant. Don't telegraph the answer by adding "or are you interested in both?" to the question.)

16. **Have you ever been tested for sales aptitude?** (If so, discuss the results.)

17. **Would your spouse or fiance be willing to attend your career interview with you?** (If so, it may be a good idea to stage a second interview; if not, there may be a problem, because salespeople must have understanding spouses. Part of your job as sales manager is not only to convince the applicant to become a salesperson, but to convince the spouse to allow it.)

18. **What distance are you willing to travel to receive professional training?** (The best time to handle an objection is before it arises. Reach an agreement on this point before going any further to save yourself and the applicant some possible inconvenience.)

19. **Suppose that to become a salesperson, it will cost you $300 to purchase a briefcase, name tag and other personal effects. If we agree on everything, will you be willing to invest $300 of your own**

money to get involved in a career? (This gives you an indication of how committed the applicant is.)

20. **If we agree on everything, when would you like to start?** (This is a good closing question.)

These are twenty good questions to give you insight into the applicant. But by no means should these necessarily be the only questions you ask. Add to this list any question you care to ask. Write down each answer.

Don't sound like a computer or a calculating personnel director when asking these questions. Act as if you're really interested. In fact, you most certainly should be interested in anyone you think has the capacity to contribute to your financial well-being.

The more you learn about the applicant and his or her abilities, the better your chances of not only saving both you and the applicant some grief later, but the better your chances of hiring a qualified salesperson.

But if you would recruit good salespeople, you'd better give them a good reason as to why they should come work for you. In fact, how would you answer the question, "Why should anyone come to work for your company?" After all, yours is not the only company through which salespeople can earn salaries. If you can't convince them of the benefits of working for your company, you'll likely lose your best prospects to the competition that has a sales manager who is able to communicate the advantages of working for his or her company.

If you don't know how to answer this question, keep reading. I'll help you find an answer in the next chapter.

IN A CAPSULE

1. There are five steps to successful interviewing. You should explain why you're hiring, describe the type of person you're seeking, ask interview questions, stage a visual presentation and schedule a second interview.

2. When applicants arrive late or on time, let them know that you've noticed. And if they arrive early, make them wait. These are control tactics.

3. Have applicants fill out applications before you give information about the job. If an applicant refuses to fill out the application before getting information, get rid of the applicant. He or she will cause you trouble.

4. Keep applications simple. Let them cover four areas—personal information, past employment, education and self-analysis, which involves the applicant stating why he or she is seeking a career in sales.

5. Applicants may be asked about their financial status. If the answer is average or below average, you may have a bad candidate.

6. After the application is completed, ask the applicant a series of approximately twenty questions designed to determine more about the applicant.

List the most important points you have gained from the
preceding Strategy:

_____

_____

_____

_____

_____

_____

_____

_____

_____

_____

_____

_____

_____

_____

_____

Strategy 7:

See Your Company As Unique

Why should anyone want to join your sales team? Try to answer that in your own mind. Is it the fact that you offer good wages? Lots of companies offer good wages. Is it the fact that your company is a good one? Lots of companies are good. You'll have to do better than that.

Why would anyone want to work for your company? I'm not trying to be difficult by asking you that question. I'm just saying that if you don't have an answer, you may let a few good prospects who ask you that same question slip right through your fingers.

People want more than a job; they want a future. They want more than a salary; they want prestige and security. You've got to convince your prospective employees that you and your company can give them what they need. Yet, many sales managers think that attracting the right people boils down to offering the salesperson a good income.

It's a common recruiting misconception that the highest incomes attract the most people. But in reality, many prospective salespeople are afraid of high incomes because they're afraid they'll receive less help from management. And in the previous chapter, I told you the three leading motivators of salespeople—**recognition, participation and sympathetic help.** For most salespeople, money as a motivator ranks no better than fourth.

Even prospective commissioned salespeople aren't enticed by commissions; they care, instead, about what they can earn on an annual basis. And also important to all prospective employees is the attitude and philosophy of the company and its manager.

In short, aside from knowing that they can earn a suitable income, prospective salespeople place a great deal of importance on whether working for your organization will be a pleasurable experience. And it's your job to convince them that it will be.

GET ENTHUSIASTIC

You wouldn't hire a salesperson who couldn't get excited about your company's product. Of course not, because an ethical salesperson can't sell something that he or she can't get excited about. Or to put it another popular way, you can't sell something you don't believe in any more than you can come back from some place you haven't been. The salesperson must be enthusiastic if he or she wants to motivate the customer to buy.

The same holds true for managers. Those who can't get excited about their companies and what they have to offer can hardly expect to motivate prospective salespeople to join their teams.

Some managers don't know the importance of enthusiasm. They don't have a clear focus on how exciting their employment situation may be to applicants. As a sales manager, you must be able to convince prospects to join your team by convincing them that your company stands out above the competition.

There are ten selling points which you can use to convince prospective salespeople that your organization has all they need to grow and prosper.

1. **Company philosophy.** One major sales organization with branches throughout the country has a unique organizational philosophy: To become successful by helping our agents become personally successful. If you can convey that, or an equally promising philosophy, to a prospective salesperson, you can score big points. Remember, prospective salespeople (like prospective buyers) always want to know what's in it for them.

2. **Objectives.** These are your company goals. If your company doesn't have any goals, the owner and/or you had better establish some, and make them crystal clear to your prospects. People need more than a job; they need a cause. They need to feel that what they're doing for a living is more than just producing a salary; they want to feel like their efforts are counting for something valuable. Money alone doesn't motivate most people, but they'll swarm like bees to get involved in a cause.

3. **History of the company.** Your better prospects are impressed with the history of your company. Why? The longer your company has been established, the less likely it is to go out of business. You can impress prospective employees by spelling out for them how and when your company started and where it is today. Prospective salespeople want to work for a company that not only came from somewhere, but also is going somewhere!

4. **Unique location.** Determine something unique about your company's location. Perhaps it has been in the

same place since it was founded, or perhaps it's located on a convenient route for customers. Perhaps it's located near a well-known landmark in your area. As a sales manager, it is important for you to determine something unique about your company's location. And it must be truly unique, because if you aren't pleased with its location, neither will your prospects be pleased.

5. **Unique method of operation.** If your company has anything unique going for it, brag about it to your prospects. This includes any unique brochures, training programs, employee aids and employee incentives.

6. **The right tools.** Perhaps your organization is equipped with a computer system that can expedite the process of making the sale. Or perhaps there are other unique tools that might entice a prospective salesperson to come to work for you. Your job is to be able to describe these tools to your prospects.

7. **Career track.** People need to know what avenues they are able to take from your organization that lead to bigger and better opportunities. If it's possible for them to work their way into management positions or other departments, let them know. Good salespeople need short-term benefits, but they also keep their eyes on long-term benefits, such as raises and promotions.

8. **Success stories from past or current employees.** Prospective employees want to know that other salespeople have done well in the employment of your company. There's no better way to show this than by offering mini-histories of past and current successful salespeople.

9. **Team concept.** Convince the prospect that the only way to sell is in a team situation. You may point out

that in other sales organizations, all the employees are below the boss; but in your organization, everyone shares in precisely the same objective and that everyone works as a team. This indicates to the prospect that he or she will play a significant role as a salesperson within your organization.

10. **Your company's unique size.** Approach this on the basis of three sizes—good, better and best. All companies are good. Some are better, and then there is the best. Yours is the best. How do I know that? The point is, you had better know that, if you want to recruit top-notch salespeople. You can't ignore the fact that there are other good places where your applicants could work. So use this fact to your advantage. Point out the good qualities of your competition, but make sure that your company comes out on top by comparison.

This could be done effectively by devising a chart that compares your company with your competition. Perhaps you can show on the chart that your company offers continuous training, a team concept, future management opportunities, above-average commissions and radio/television/newspaper advertisements. Perhaps the competition will only offer some of those qualities.

Or perhaps you might point out that all companies are good, but a few are better than others, and still fewer qualify as the best. For example, let's take three types of companies. Company A is an independent, individually-owned sales office with a nice personal atmosphere. Employees will get a great deal of personal attention. Company B is part of a national chain of offices. Employees there will be part of a strong national organization. Company C is an individually-owned franchise of a national sales organization, which combines, more or less, the best of both worlds.

Which company is the best? Which company is yours? I could sit down and tell you how all three companies are the best. If you go to work for Company A, not only will you get a lot of attention, but you won't get lost in the sea of anonymity that employees of Company B (and to some extent, Company C) must swim. That makes Company A the best. Yet, employees of Company B may enjoy a greater image in the marketplace because of the chain affiliation, not to mention the fact that the chain company may be financially stronger than the individually-owned company. That would make Company B the best. Of course, since Company C offers the best of both worlds, its selling point should be clear.

A good recruiter must know how to sell, because the recruiter must "sell" the benefits of his or her company to the prospective salespeople.

GET VISUAL

As I told you before, there are sales managers who, as salespeople, enthusiastically stage visual presentations for buyers to better their chances of getting the orders. Yet, as sales managers, they won't take the time to stage one for an applicant who has the potential to bring the company thousands upon thousands of orders over the years.

Why is a visual presentation so important? Because studies show that people remember far more of what they see than what they hear. A visual image, along with your words, will make a greater impact on the receiver of your message.

94

Willie Sutton, the most prolific bank robber in world history, subscribed fully to the use of visuals. When asked why he used a gun to rob banks, which compounded the felony indeed, Sutton reportedly replied, "Because I found early in my career that a visual aid and a few well chosen words got me much farther than just the words alone. The words, 'Stick 'em up,' just didn't carry the proper weight without the visual aid."

I really feel that the visual presentation is a very important part of the first interview, because you will lose applicants who aren't "sold" on you, your organization, your business and on their own abilities to sell, and you'll never know why.

So now it's time to make this applicant desire to become involved with you and your company and the sales business. And a visual presentation is great for this. With a visual presentation, you can accomplish four things, including:

1. **Getting the applicant to participate.**

2. **Keeping the applicant interested.**

3. **Getting mini-commitments from the applicant.**

4. **Keeping control of the presentation.**

The sales manager who asks questions of the applicant while staging the visual presentation will accomplish all four of these points. A person who asks questions is always in control, and the person answering them is always most interested. The applicant who answers questions is participating, and he or she will give mini-commitments to properly worded tie-down questions. I'll explain that point further in a few more paragraphs.

But in the meantime, you might start your presentation by saying something to this effect: "I certainly feel I have a clear picture of you, and quite frankly, I'm impressed. I think we can work well together. I'm sure you have questions, so let me go over a presentation that I think will help answer any questions you may have."

95

Then tell the applicant that most people considering career changes usually have three questions to ask:

1. **Why should I consider a career in sales?**

2. **Why should I join this company as opposed to hundreds of others?**

3. **Do I have what it takes?**

Keep the presentation simple. Make sure you cover the basic points of your message with pictures. For example, why should a person consider a sales career? There are many benefits, including flexible hours, unlimited earnings (in the case of commissioned salespeople), equal opportunity, exciting product (all products are exciting, of course, with the possible exception of hula hoops and pogo sticks) and continuing employment.

Each point should be accompanied by a visual aid of sorts. For example, when you reach the part about flexible hours, you might show a picture that shows a person pursuing a personal hobby; unlimited earnings (if applicable) could be illustrated with a picture of several stacks of legal tender and several bulging bank bags; equal opportunity can be illustrated with a picture of an assembly of people of all ages, sexes and races; your exciting product can be illustrated, of course, with a picture of the product, if not the product itself; and continuing employment can best be illustrated with a picture of an employment office with a circle around it and a slash through it.

As you cover each point, you might explain it by saying, "One of the reasons that many people consider sales as a career is because of flexible hours. Unlike a lot of careers, if you want to take your time off to enjoy your family or hobbies, you can do it. As long as you're productive and participating, you can choose your own hours. Of course, the more hours you work, the more money you'll get paid. But I'm going to give you a career where you can be your own boss."

Of course, you would handle the other points similarly. The more sales a salesperson makes, the more he or she will likely earn, either through commissions or (for non-commissioned salespeople) bonuses and/or salary increases for good performances. People of all ages, races and sexes may be salespeople, and no hard-working, productive salesperson ever got laid off when the economy was down.

And after you've covered each point, ask your applicant a good tie-down question, such as, "Does flexible hours (unlimited earnings, equal opportunity, continuing employment, etc.) sound good to you?" Naturally, the applicant will agree, and this helps create an "atmosphere of agreement" that will help convince the applicant to come to work for your company.

As for describing your exciting product and why the applicant should consider your company, I think you're well qualified to do that. If you have trouble with that, refer to the ten selling points mentioned earlier.

But then, there's the applicant's question, "Do I have what it takes?" Point out that there are three ways to succeed in the sales business:

1. **Personal experience, which is time-consuming and results in a lot of mistakes;**

2. **Personal research, which also takes a lot of time;**

3. **Being trained by the organization for which an applicant is employed.**

You should offer the applicant option number three. And if your company doesn't employ a field trainer, then it's costing itself money. The office that doesn't offer training in this day and age when consumers are more sophisticated and educated than ever shouldn't be in business. And it probably won't stay in business for long, because the sales business is getting too complex. Even if the field training program consists of only audio cassettes or one-on-one instruction, there should be a training program of some type.

Then there are other questions you may ask to help the applicant answer in his or her own mind whether he or she has "what it takes." And these questions also may be illustrated with pictures, such as:

1. **"Are you a team player?"** Salespeople must be team players to succeed. Occasionally, for example, you might be asked to handle some extra time on the telephone.

2. **"Do you like people?"** If you just work for money, you're heading for failure. But if you are willing to help people because you care about them, then you'll succeed in the sales business. You've got to like people. Do everything they expect, plus a little more because you like them.

3. **"Do you want an above-average income?"** If you're just looking for an average-paying job, then sales is not for you. If you're satisfied with less, then sales is not for you.

4. **"Are you a self-starter?"** You've got to be your own motivator. Your own initiative has got to motivate you to get out and meet people. If you don't have that desire, you won't succeed.

Remember, during your visual presentation, feel free to "blow your own horn," so to speak. Actually, you're trying to convince the applicant to come to work for your company and, more personally, you. The better the presentation you stage, the better your chances of convincing that applicant to join your team.

OFFER AN APTITUDE TEST

After you've staged your visual presentation, you should conclude the interview by offering the applicant an aptitude test or personality profile. This is to give you more information about the applicant while creating in the applicant's mind that you're being very selective about who you hire. And if a person really thinks you have a super selection process, they'll be willing to sacrifice a lot to join your team.

Remember what I said earlier about the U.S. Marines? Their basic training is second to none in exhausting physical demands. They're usually the first to arrive at world trouble spots and they're usually the first to die if the situation involves combat. And despite all this, the pay is no higher for Marines than it is for any other branch of the armed services. Yet, the Marines virtually always have a backlog of recruits who are just waiting to get in. The reason is because the Marines have developed a "super-selection" process with such slogans as "The Few, The Proud, The Marines" and "We're Looking For A Few Good Men."

So ask the applicant to take an aptitude test, making it clear that the decision to hire will not be based on the test alone. After all, I've never found an aptitude test that can tell you whether a person will make it in sales. Years ago, I failed an aptitude test to be an instructor in the Navy; I also failed an aptitude test to be a salesman for a life insurance company. I don't think aptitude tests are very good gauges; instead, I think they're good for more information.

Do not discuss salary and/or commissions with the applicant, because the last thing you want is for the applicant to shop around for the best salary offer or commission structure. (Most people don't care about commission structures as much as they care about what they can reasonably earn on an annual basis.)

Besides, income is to be discussed later. This will help motivate the applicant to come back for the second interview. I'll cover it in the next chapter.

IN A CAPSULE

1. If you can't communicate to applicants why they should work for your company above all others, then you may lose some good qualified applicants. Learn how to "sell" applicants on your company by citing its positive, lucrative and pleasurable benefits.

2. Be enthusiastic about the ten selling points of your company. They should include the company's philosophy, objectives, history, unique location, unique method of operation, special tools, success stories, team concept and unique size.

3. Good sales managers will stage visual presentations to help "sell" applicants on their organizations. After all, a point can be made much better with words and visuals than with just words alone.

4. Visual presentations allow applicants to participate and maintain interest in the interview process. They also get mini-commitments from the applicants and allow the sales manager to maintain control of the interview.

5. Visual presentations should answer three questions for the applicant.
   a. Why should I consider a career in sales?
   b. Why should I join this company as opposed to hundreds of others?
   c. Do I have what it takes?

6. The benefits to a sales career are flexible hours, equal employment, exciting product (all products are exciting, of course), unlimited earnings (for commissioned salespeople) and continuing employment.

7. An applicant who wants to know if he or she has what it takes to succeed should be asked four questions:
   a. Are you a team player?
   b. Do you like people?
   c. Do you want an above-average income?
   d. Are you a self-starter?

8. Conclude the first interview with an aptitude test to obtain more information about the applicant. But you shouldn't base your decision on whether or not to hire on the test alone. They're not infallible.

List the most important points you have gained from the
preceding Strategy:

_____

_____

_____

_____

_____

_____

_____

_____

_____

_____

_____

_____

_____

_____

_____

_____

Strategy 8:

Successful Selection and Second Interview

You can't judge a person by the way he or she dresses, although dress does make a difference. You also can't evaluate a person by his or her ability to communicate, although communication counts for something. Success can neither be measured nor predicted by the way a person stands, sits and walks, although posture is most important to a positive, pleasing image. You also can't tell whether a person will persevere by his or her personality, although personality is a factor that shouldn't be taken lightly.

So how can you tell whether a person applying for a sales position has what it takes to succeed? You can't. Not for certain, anyway.

Too many managers tend to look at the person for the answer. If he or she looks good, communicates well, stands erect and has an outgoing personality, they may say, "Hey, look at that person. I think he/she will do well."

But they don't know it for certain. They won't know it until after the person has had a chance to prove him/herself. In fact, that's when managers truly learn whether salespeople have what it takes to succeed—when they have proven, or failed to prove, themselves.

IT'S WHAT'S INSIDE THAT COUNTS

Untold numbers of sales managers and business owners have invested unlimited funds each year in various selection processes, (a series of aptitude and personality profile exams that investigate individuals,) only to find that the individual will only be as good as he/she is trainable.

I think managers spend too much time looking for the perfect characteristic. I believe there are many misconceptions about what qualities should be sought in a prospective salesperson. If you believe what you read, many self-made successful people say that everyone has what it takes to succeed if he or she is willing to pay the price. And you can't determine whether a person is willing to pay the price with only a superficial glimpse of the person.

It's like the story about the salesman who sold helium-filled balloons on a busy street corner. When business tended to stall, the salesman would release a balloon into the sky to draw attention to his business.

Over the course of the day, balloons of all colors ascended into the air—yellows, reds, blues, greens, oranges and pinks. And not too far from the salesman was a little black boy, who had eagerly watched each balloon rise into the heavens.

Finally, the little boy approached the balloon salesman. "Mister," he said. "If you let go of a black balloon, would it rise like the others?"

The salesman must have been sensitive indeed, for with the

wisdom of the ages, he said, "Son, the color of the balloons is not important. It's what is inside that makes the difference."

And that's the way it is with salespeople. An attractive appearance, a good personality, an ability to communicate well and good posture can be positive benefits.

But all those attributes can be compared with icing on a cake. The cake itself is comparable to the skills that make a salesperson successful.

ICING IS NICE, BUT IT ISN'T ENOUGH

I can personally attest to the fact that successful salespeople are more than just attractive, articulate, interesting and poised. As living proof of this, I submit to you one Domonico Siciliano, a citizen of Italian descent who answered a recruiting ad I ran for a real estate office in Pleasant Ridge, Michigan.

I took one look at Domonico and decided within ten seconds that there was no way I was going to hire him. His state of dress left something to be desired and his posture was poor, making for an overall shabby appearance. And as for his personality? I couldn't tell, because Domonico didn't speak English! At least, he didn't speak it as well as a real estate agent should, I thought.

But Domonico was persistent, and I finally decided to give him a chance (not so much because I thought he would succeed, but because it was the only way to get rid of him). I assumed that he lacked the knowledge of the English language to pass the real estate exam.

But he did pass. He had to take the test four times, but he passed. And his first year in business, Domonico Siciliano closed ninety-four transactions! That was more than six times the business that the average first-year real estate agent generated.

Domonico taught me that looking good is not a requirement

for success. After all, between clothes, weight-loss programs, weight-gain products, cosmetics and hair dye, anybody can look good.

And as for having an outgoing personality, let me introduce you to a young lady I met as a real estate sales consultant. She was the most introverted person you'd ever want to meet. She didn't talk; she mumbled. She was one of the most bashful people I had ever met.

But, boy, could she ever sell real estate! Her first year in business, she sold $1 million in real estate; her second year, $2 million; her third, $3 million; her fourth, $4 million; her fifth, $6.6 million; her sixth, $7.2 million. And these sales totals reflected a period of time when the average home on the market sold for $50,000!

My point, dear sales manager, is to be careful about what you look for in potential salespeople. The people who succeed in the sales business are industrious; they are people who like to win. They are achievers, because they are competitive. And they have a need or want for money.

Industrious, achievers and money. Put together the first letters of each word and you get the words, "I am." If your applicant is an industrious achiever with a strong desire or need for money, hire the applicant; you can teach him or her how to dress, communicate and stand later.

HOW DO YOU LOOK
FOR WHAT YOU CAN'T SEE?

If a sales manager interviews an applicant and asks if he or she is a hard worker, how do you think the applicant will respond? Of course, the applicant will say, "Oh, yeah, I'm a hard worker."

And if the manager asks if he or she is an achiever, how do you think the applicant will respond to that? "Oh, yeah, I'm one of the best achievers around."

Then the manager undoubtedly will ask the applicant if he or she has a strong desire and/or need for money. And, of course, we know how the applicant should answer, because frankly, I've met very few people who didn't need, or at least couldn't use, more money.

So the manager hires the applicant, thinking, "Hot Dog! I've got a winner." And yet, that "winner" falls flat on his or her face during a dismal probationary period.

Did the manager make a bad selection? Of course. Instead of asking if the applicant was a hard worker, an achiever and in need of money, the manager would have been better off to ask the questions recommended in the previous chapter. "What have you done in the past to prove that you are a hard worker? That you are an achiever? That you want or need money?" This puts the monkey on the back of the applicant, where it rightfully belongs. After all, the manager "sells" the applicant on the company; the employee should be expected to "sell" him or herself to the manager.

YOU CAN'T SELECT UNTIL AFTER YOU HIRE

But let's not be too hard on the manager for making a faulty selection. After all, the word "selection" should be put to rest right now in relation to the hiring process, because "selection" doesn't occur until long after the applicant has been hired and has started working. A manager doesn't "select" an applicant to become a bona fide salesperson until after the applicant has worked through a probationary period. I don't think any manager knows in advance whether or not an applicant will succeed.

All the manager can do during the interview process is make "mini-selections." And the more of those the manager can make, the better the chances of the applicant succeeding. For example, suppose a manager stages a first interview with someone who seems to have all the traits of a salesperson, but none of the appearance. Perhaps the hair length and the state of dress is unacceptable.

If the applicant is otherwise unobjectionable, the manager may then state his or her objections to the applicant and ask if the applicant can return for the second interview with trimmed hair and upgraded attire. If, on the second interview, the applicant complies with the manager's requests, then the manager has a good idea that the applicant can take direction—a positive trait for any salesperson.

Then, the manager can make a "mini-selection" in favor of the applicant. But the true selection comes after the fact. Unless the manager has a reliable crystal ball, there is no way he or she can determine in advance whether an applicant will be able to succeed.

YOU CAN HIRE IF YOU'RE WILLING TO FIRE

I once interviewed a casually-dressed applicant with long hair and a beard and absolutely no sales experience. I asked him to clean up his act before he came back for a second interview. He returned with trimmed hair, no beard and a three-piece suit. During his first year, he sold $1.5 million in real estate. I also gave a chance to a seventy-plus-year-old grandmother, who also didn't disappoint me.

You can give anyone a chance at sales, provided that you're willing to fire if the person can't meet your minimum standards.

On the other hand, don't overdo the selection process. Although you want to project selectivity, you don't want to become too selective, or else you'll pass over many qualified potential salespeople. Again, I believe anyone can succeed in selling, if he or she is willing to pay the price and take direction.

Besides, selection is a two-way street. Your applicant also will be making a selection decision. Your appearance is very important, because you are the living embodiment of the sales business to the applicant. You are what the applicant envisions himself or herself becoming.

It's very important that managers not only dress for success, but that their offices radiate a successful appearance. If there is junk piled on every chair, that indicates a negative appearance. If the desk is so cluttered that Sherlock Holmes couldn't find the desktop, that indicates a negative, disorganized appearance.

It's also important for a manager to communicate well, because managers must sound successful if they would "sell" success to applicants. Another reason it is vitally important to stage a good presentation in every respect is because the applicant, if married, must "sell" you and your company to his or her spouse. That's why it's important for the spouse to attend the second interview, if at all possible.

INVESTIGATE APPLICANTS

I've been burned more times than I care to remember because I didn't ask applicants to list their previous employers. If you don't do this already, start a good habit. It's not an unreasonable demand, and it can save you a lot of headaches later.

Then, of course, call those former employers and ask them two questions:

1. **How would you describe the applicant?**

2. **Would you rehire the applicant? Why?**

Listen to both answers. Of course, investigation doesn't need to stop there. If you believe your applicant has a shaky financial background, run a credit check on him or her. It can't hurt; it can only enlighten you.

Generally, it takes three things to make the best initial selection possible—instinct, good communication and information.

First, trust your instincts; they're usually correct. If you feel uncomfortable with an applicant, decide negative. Second, good communication is essential. Tell your applicants what you expect of them, and find out if they're willing to give you positive answers. And third, weigh the information that you gather from the applicant. How does it sound? Is this the type of person you want to return for a second interview?

If you're a truly busy sales manager, you should never conduct a second interview with anyone you're not willing to hire for any reason. There is no point to wasting your time or the applicant's time. Simply telephone the applicant and state up front that you're not interested at this time. Tell the applicant that he or she has some good points and ask permission to call back if the situation should change.

And before you hang up the phone, ask the applicant if he or she is interested, or knows anyone else who might be interested, in buying whatever it is you have to sell. It can't hurt.

On the other hand, if you do want the applicant to return for a second interview, call and schedule an appointment.

THE SECOND INTERVIEW

Remember, you didn't discuss money with the applicant during the first interview for two reasons. One, you wanted the applicant to think about sales itself as a career and to determine if he or she would be interested in working with you. And two, you didn't want the potential salesperson shopping around for the best compensation.

So conducting the second interview is simple. First, review the applicant's aptitude or personality test results. Consult with the applicant on any weak points, such as, "The test indicates you need direction; how well do you take direction?"

Then, get ready to discuss money, because now you're going to answer any questions from the applicant, or iron out the details. You might begin by saying, "On our last visit, I discussed with you the benefits of a sales career, what a person must have to succeed and why you should work for our company. I don't think you would be here today if I hadn't convinced you on each of those points.

"So now, let's talk about earnings. Here is a list of people who, at one time or another, were sitting in the same chair that you occupy. Like you, they were as green as grass when it came to sales. Now here is one man, a former boilermaker, who did well starting out. And here is a lady who . . . ."

Impress the applicant with the average production of your success stories. Don't "blue sky" the applicants, or promise them the world. You'll only demoralize them later if their earnings fail to meet your announced expectations.

I have recruited and hired hundreds of people with this system. I've learned that people are more concerned with short-term earnings than they are with long-term potential earnings. They want to know if the manager is blue-skying them, or if other people have actually made similar earnings.

Your job as manager is to paint a lucrative, but truthful, portrait of what they can expect—provided that they're willing to do their part to get it.

NEGATIVES WILL ARISE

Suppose your applicant informs you that another company in the area pays more than your company. That, in itself, is an objection from the applicant. The applicant wants to know why he or she should work for you if greater compensation can be obtained elsewhere.

All salespeople—whether they are sales managers or door-to-door peddlers—should be able to turn negatives into positives. Simply respond by saying, "Yes, that's true. But there are two things I want you to think about. Number one, why do you suppose some companies must offer greater compensation? It might be because they don't have as much to offer in terms of guidance and training. The difference between what they have to offer and what we have to offer can make the difference between success and failure."

At this point, you might consult your list of successes again to illustrate that a large number of people fail in the sales business, while a large percentage of your salespeople succeed.

Again, it's not what you pay that is important; instead, it's the fact that you can help show people how to make a good living.

Will you lose any of your prospects on the second interview? Of course. But prospects who consider compensation to be the most important factor of the business eventually will leave you anyway. In that case, it's better to lose them at the beginning.

WRAPPING UP LOOSE ENDS

In the case of real estate and other salespeople who must be licensed to sell, the next step is to enroll the salesperson into a pre-licensing school. During the course of the training, it's important to follow-up with the applicant. Contact the applicant once a week, and ask how the studies are going. But don't offer to help them. After all, the instructor probably knows more about the topic than you do. You might confuse your applicant, which could be disastrous at exam time. And don't insist that they come in every day to learn the business, because if they've failed the exam, you've wasted thousands of dollars worth of your time.

Just remember, it's what you do with your salespeople during their first two months in the sales business that will determine how they'll fare for the remainder of their careers.

But keep the applicants involved somewhat in the business between hiring and passing of the exam. Invite them to positive meetings, contests, kick-offs, motivational meetings and rallies. Keep them away from normal sales meetings for the time being.

Of course, for most salespeople, no licensing is required. So when you and the applicant agree on terms, shake hands and welcome your new salesperson aboard. It can be the start of a very good relationship.

IN A CAPSULE

1. In the process of hiring, sales managers generally won't know whether a person has what it takes to succeed until after the person has had a chance to prove himself or herself.

2. Looking good and sounding good is not enough to succeed in the sales business. Regardless of what a salesperson looks like, he or she will be likely to succeed if he or she is industrious, achievement-oriented and competitive. And they must also need or want money.

3. When interviewing an applicant, make him or her prove to you why he or she is a hard worker, is an achiever and has a strong desire or need for money. This gives the applicant a chance to "sell" himself or herself to the sales manager.

4. If there is something about an applicant that is objectionable, a sales manager can communicate this objection to the applicant at the first interview with the advice that he or she overcome the objection by the second interview. If the applicant overcomes the objection, the sales manager has a good idea that the applicant can take direction.

5. You can give anyone a chance at a sales career, provided that you're willing to fire that person if he or she can't meet your minimum standards.

6. Selection is a two-way street. Your applicant will be selecting—or rejecting—you. Your appearance must make a good impression on the applicant, because you will be what the applicant envisions himself or herself becoming. To maximize the first impression, you should communicate well and your office should be presentable, also.

7. Always get references and check them to avoid possible problems later. Ask former employers two questions: How would you describe the applicant? Would you rehire the applicant and why?

8. Trust your instincts. If you feel uncomfortable with an applicant, decide negative.

9. Good communication is essential. Tell your applicants what you expect of them, and find out if they're willing to give you positive answers.

10. Weigh the information you gather from the applicant. How does it sound? Is this the type of person you want to return for a second interview? If not, contact the person and state up front that you're not interested at this time. Tell the applicant that he or she has some good points and ask permission to call back if the situation should change. If it is a person you would like to see again, call and schedule a second interview.

11. During the second interviews, sales managers should paint for applicants a lucrative, but truthful, portrait of what financial rewards and benefits they can expect over the years, provided that the applicants are willing to do their part.

12. Applicants who point out that a competitor offers greater compensation should be told that perhaps the competitor doesn't offer the training and guidance that your company offers. You might show how a large number of people fail in the sales business, while a large percentage of your salespeople succeed.

13. Remember, it's what you do with your salespeople during their first two months in the sales business that will determine how they'll fare for the remainder of their careers.

List the most important points you have gained from the
preceding Strategy:

_____

_____

_____

_____

_____

_____

_____

_____

_____

_____

_____

_____

_____

_____

_____

_____

NOTES

Section 3

TRAINING

Strategy 9:

Mastering the Eleven Principles of Training

This chapter must be generalized to be of benefit to all the sales managers who read it. Obviously, I can't offer a training program that would suit the needs of every sales manager of every different sales operation in North America. Aside from the fact that there isn't enough space in the book, I'd be stepping out of my realm of expertise if I were to set myself up as an expert on, say, the field of automobile sales.

But, for the good news, selling is selling is selling. I've long contended that a real estate agent could know virtually nothing about real estate, yet still succeed as long as he or she knew how to sell. By the same token, I've also long contended that an agent who knew everything about real estate, but nothing about sales, would eventually starve out of the business.

This is true because whether you sell real estate, automobiles, insurance, furniture or widgets, the process of selling is virtually the same. Certain thoughts must develop in the prospective buyer's mind before he or she will buy, and salespeople, in a sense, must know how to help said thoughts develop.

When you've reached the point where you can lead a team of salespeople, you undoubtedly will be able to teach your salespeople how to function. You don't need my help in that area. But don't skip on to the next chapter just yet, because I still may be of benefit to you.

As I've said, I can't give you specific "how-to's" pertaining to every varied sales operation there is, but I can give you some strong training principles that can be applied to every type of sales business. If you follow these principles, I believe you'll find that your salespeople will function to maximum efficiency and effectiveness, and that should be good news, indeed.

PRINCIPLE NUMBER ONE:

BASICS FIRST, FINER POINTS LATER

The first rule of training salespeople is to make them strong at the basics first, then train them in areas of specialty.

In the military, there are all types of assignments for young men and women. Some may be translators, others may be technicians. Some may be in infantry, others may be in medicine. Some may be mechanics, and still others may be musicians.

Despite the varied occupations and assignments of U.S. service men and women, they share one point in common: All of them must first complete basic training. Before they can advance to any area of expertise, they must first become strong at the basics. No matter what job they might hold, the time very well may come when they will be pressed into service as soldiers. Therefore, it is imperative that they be effectively trained to serve in that capacity. For that reason, the basic training process—or "boot camp"—hasn't been changed throughout the years.

It doesn't matter what you're selling; when it gets down to the heart of the matter, the process is the same for your salespeople and the salespeople who sell widgets.

Therefore, you should make your salespeople strong at the basics first. After they've mastered the basics, their success rate in more specialized training can't help but be improved.

PRINCIPLE NUMBER TWO:

MAKE CONTACTS WITH STRANGERS

In any type of sales business, the most basic "basic" is to make contacts with strangers.

No matter what you're selling, if you seek prospective customers from only your friends or people you know, you'll eventually starve out of the sales business. I don't care how many people a salesperson knows, it simply won't be enough to support the salesperson.

The success of any salesperson is in direct response to his or her willingness to make contacts with total strangers. If you can instill this principle in your salespeople, you will have given them the basic tool that all salespeople must have to survive in the sales business.

PRINCIPLE NUMBER THREE:

MAKE THEM INDEPENDENT

In the "Manager's Manual" discussed earlier, I advised you to make your salespeople independent of you, not dependent upon you. This principle bears repeating. Aside from the fact that dependent salespeople will consume more of your time than it may be possible for you to give, this principle is worth teaching for another reason: Until they become independent, they'll never be good salespeople.

Have you ever wondered why people under the care of psychiatrists are so devoted to them? It's because the psychiatrists are teaching the people how to stand on their own two feet. They earn the respect of their patients because they help them become independent. If you make your salespeople independent of you, you'll teach them confidence, which will lead to independence. In so doing, you'll earn their respect, and, in gratitude, they'll be likely to "go to war" for you when you need them most. Allow them to remain dependent, and they eventually will drive you crazy.

PRINCIPLE NUMBER FOUR:

MAKE THEM GOOD; DON'T LET THEM BE BAD

When we talked about minimum standards, I pointed out that your salespeople will be as good or as bad as you train or allow them to be. If you have a poor producer on your team who has been a poor producer for more months than you care to remember, you must accept at least some of the blame. Either your training of this salesperson was deficient, or you have allowed him or her to remain on the team, despite his or her poor production.

When you allow salespeople to fall below your minimum standards, you are sending a message to the other members of your team that poor performance will be accepted. This will remove some of the "healthy pressure" that inspires them to perform well. As a result, you eventually may have three or four poor producers instead of just one.

PRINCIPLE NUMBER FIVE:

ASSUME THEY DON'T KNOW

If a salesperson is having trouble with a particular element of sales, always assume that he or she doesn't know the correct procedure. Then show them. When you assume that the salesperson does know the correct procedure, the salesperson is likely to profess to know it, rather than risk embarrassment among his or her peers by professing ignorance. Of course, such a situation is not conducive to learning.

Always assume the salesperson doesn't know the correct technique, and willingly demonstrate it for the salesperson.

There's an old slogan that I once read on a milk carton. It may be the best information I've ever gotten from a milk carton, because there's a world of truth in it. I'll share it with you: I hear and I forget. I see and I remember. I do and I understand.

When your salespeople are slow to learn or having trouble remembering, make them role play the situation. It's essential to the learning process, because the more they do something, even in a simulated situation, the easier it will be for them to master it.

PRINCIPLE NUMBER SIX:

BE A GOOD EXAMPLE

Your salespeople will do as you do, not as you say. Don't try to teach them human relation skills if you're known as the office grouch. Your effort will be wasted. If you teach them to be organized, make sure that you and your office are in order. If your office looks like a cyclone passed through it, you'll be advertising the fact that you lack credibility.

If you would teach, you must practice what you preach. If you don't, you'll fail at teaching, because just as actions speak louder than words, examples teach better than instructions.

If you would have your salespeople "look the part," you'd better be no slouch yourself. If you would have them communicate well, there had better be nothing ambiguous or unclear about what you tell them. And above all, if you would teach them to listen well, you'd better be pretty good at it yourself.

Salespeople need more than just being told what to do. They need to see how such principles can contribute positively to their careers. The sales manager who adopts such principles before teaching them serves as the best example. The sales manager who preaches but doesn't practice serves as no example at all.

PRINCIPLE NUMBER SEVEN:

A LITTLE BIT AT A TIME

Teach your salespeople well, but don't teach them too much, too soon. It takes time for a principle learned to become instilled in a person to the point that it becomes second nature. For example, a child doesn't learn to write words immediately after learning how to talk. First, the child must learn the alphabet. After mastering that, the child must learn to read. From reading, the child must become a speller. After the child has mastered spelling, then he or she may learn to write.

"Space training" is most essential for new salespeople. In other words, you should teach them, then leave them alone for a while so they can become fully familiar with what they have learned. Only after they have mastered one point should they be introduced to other points.

PRINCIPLE NUMBER EIGHT:

GIVE REFRESHER TRAINING

Even the best training in the world will go stale if you don't offer refresher training to your salespeople. The longer salespeople stay in the business without refresher training, the farther they get away from the basics.

It's not at all uncommon to see salespeople succeed in their first year of business, only to watch them fall into a slump during their second year because they got away from the basics.

Let's draw an analogy between the conscious mind and a barrel of water. After the water reaches a capacity point in the barrel, some water will spill over the sides if more water is introduced to the barrel. By the same token, everything we learn is stored in the conscious mind until a capacity point is reached. At that point, for every new thing learned, an old point is forgotten.

That's why refresher training is imperative, especially with people who have been in the business for ten years or more. The longer a salesperson has been in the business, the more likely he or she is going to need refresher training.

So, after you teach, don't assume they'll remember forever. Give them a break. Get them back to basics periodically with refresher training.

PRINCIPLE NUMBER NINE:

CLASS AND FIELD TRAINING IS NECESSARY

There is quite a difference between classroom and field training. Classroom instruction prepares a student for reality, while field training is reality under supervision. Make no mistake, your salespeople need both.

I can think of no better example to illustrate my point than that of drivers' training. Students first must undergo classroom instruction that teaches them all about how to operate a car, from switching on the ignition, disengaging the clutch, putting the car into gear and depressing the accelerator. Of course, the instruction also focuses on driving on the right side of the road and the importance of staying within the speed limit.

But God help the young driver and the motoring public as well if we put him or her on the road without any viable field training. You can be taught the correct procedure for making a right turn from now until doomsday, but you won't learn as effectively as you will once you've experienced reality by running over a curb!

Classroom instruction prepares your salespeople for reality. It mixes concepts and discussion with customizing for individual needs.

132

Field training is the reality with which they need to become familiar to survive.

Can you imagine what would happen to would-be swimmers who aced all written examinations on the sport, yet had never actually been in the water? The first time they actually took the plunge, they would quickly find out first-hand that they didn't know all they needed to survive.

Classroom instruction is not enough. Your salespeople also will need field training before they can become independent and efficient. See that they get it.

PRINCIPLE NUMBER TEN:

SUBSCRIBE TO A TRAINING PROCESS

Exactly what you teach your salespeople depends on what your company sells. But I've got a training process that will work for you, no matter what you sell.

First, tell your salespeople what you intend to tell them during the class session. Then tell them. Then show them. Then give them the chance to do it, and then critique them. Then watch them do it again, and critique them. Then watch them do it one more time, then critique them. Keep repeating the last two steps until the salesperson gets it right.

Remember, role playing is essential for learning. Your salespeople will only be as good or as bad as you train or allow them to be. Make sure they learn the correct methods, then they'll be able to take care of themselves.

PRINCIPLE NUMBER ELEVEN:

PLAY IT AGAIN, SALESPERSON

Socrates first pointed out that the key to learning anything is through repetition. How did you learn the alphabet? By repeating it to yourself over and over again until you got it right. How did you learn your multiplication tables? By repeating them to yourself over and over again until you got them right. If you ever had to memorize a Shakespearean sonnet, the Gettysburg Address or the preamble to the United States Constitution, how did you learn? By repeating it to yourself until you got it right.

For that reason alone, the sales manager who doesn't encourage audio cassette tape learning systems is costing himself or herself money and is causing more grief than is necessary for his or her job.

Cassette tapes for sales instruction are the perfect tools because a well-prepared plan of instruction preserved on audio tape can accomplish several objectives:

1. **Greater Understanding Of Material.** Not only can the lesson plan be learned at a time that is most suitable to the salesperson, but the tape can be replayed if the salesperson misses a particular point.

2. **Greater Consistency of Material.** An instructor's moods may affect what he or she teaches, since moods could affect his or her ability to communicate. But cassette tapes play the same message, day in and day out.

3. **Saves Sales Manager's Time.** Aside from the fact that the manager's teaching time in the classroom is reduced, the manager also can save time by offering the cassette

tape to a salesperson who needs a second explanation of the process.

4. **Cassettes are best suited and most conducive to learning.** Sales managers often don't have time to teach, let alone to drill. But a salesperson can replay a cassette tape dozens of times for maximum advantage.

It has been said that audio cassette tapes are the best and least expensive private tutors available. No human being has as much patience as a cassette player. A particular point can be reviewed on tapes literally dozens of times, and no one is going to lose his or her temper. The cost of a cassette learning system, when broken down to actual use, can amount to nothing more than mere pennies, especially if the instruction program is self-recorded. You won't find a human instructor who will work for so little.

A LITTLE SPECIALIZED ADVICE

Again, I can't give you "how-to" advice in this chapter. But now that I've sold you (I hope) on the concept of cassette learning systems, I can at least introduce you to certain experts who indeed can help you with what you need to know to get the most out of your sales force.

These people whom I will recommend are indeed experts. They rate among the country's great sales trainers. Their cassette systems have been used by sales managers and salespeople throughout the country. If you haven't used similar systems already, I would heartily advise you to consider seriously implementing such a system.

For general and corporate sales, I would recommend Nido Qubein, a keynote speaker, business consultant and sales trainer who has taught thousands of salespeople in hundreds of seminars he has conducted around the world.

For general and real estate sales, allow me to recommend myself, Ed Escobar or Mike Ferry, all top real estate sales trainers and business consultants. Automobile salespeople might learn from Jackie Coogan (noted speaker, not the late actor), and insurance agents could be helped by speaker Joe Gandolpho of the insurance industry.

Zig Ziglar offers great cassette learning systems for general sales and closing techniques instruction, and so does Tom Hopkins. Roger Dawson's tapes on negotiating techniques will help anyone who needs help in that department. Fine multi-level marketing instruction can be obtained from David Stewart, Dave Johnson and Steven Cates.

Of course, there are many different cassette tape systems from which to choose. These are just some of the best.

Over a quarter of a million Floyd Wickman audio/visual cassettes are being used throughout North America. Topics include:

Sales, motivation, goal setting, telephone techniques, time management, objection handling and management techniques.

For further information, call or write to:

Floyd Wickman Associates
2119 E. Fourteen Mile Road
Sterling Heights, MI 48310
(313) 978-1900

IN A CAPSULE

1. Make your salespeople strong in the basics first. Once the basics become second nature to them, they'll be ready to learn and master the finer points.

2. The most basic rule of all basic rules for salespeople is to be willing to make contacts with strangers. No selling business can survive, let alone thrive, if the salespeople limit their contacts to people they know.

3. Make your salespeople independent of you, not dependent on you. Aside from the fact that you'll save time, you'll also make your salespeople more confident and, as a result, more efficient if you teach them how to stand on their own feet.

4. Your salespeople will only be as good or bad as you train or allow them to be. If you have poor producers, the fault may be in the training. If it is, correct it. Make your salespeople role play certain selling situations to strengthen them in the basics. If the fault isn't in the training, perhaps the poor producers should be eliminated. If you allow them to remain on the team, you'll, in effect, lower your standards, and the remaining team members will notice.

5. If you teach, practice what you preach. Your salespeople will pay more attention to the principles you espouse if you practice them. Don't expect them to be organized if you're not. Don't expect them to develop good human relation skills if you haven't developed any yourself.

6. Don't teach your salespeople too much too soon. Let them get strong at each point they learn before introducing them to another.

7. Give refresher training periodically. Even your best sales-people will get away from the basics the longer they stay in the sales business.

8. Start a good training process by telling your salespeople what you intend to teach them, teach them, then show them. Then have them role play the situation and watch, then critique them. Repeat the last two steps until they get it right.

9. Repetitive learning is the best way to learn anything. Audio cassette tapes are invaluable tools for teaching. They're efficient, effective and, most of all, inexpensive, especially if the tapes are self-recorded.

10. Advice for specialized sales tapes can be obtained by writing or calling Floyd Wickman Associates, 2119 E. Fourteen Mile Road, Sterling Heights, MI 48310, tele-phone 313-978-1900.

List the most important points you have gained from the
preceding Strategy:

_____

_____

_____

_____

_____

_____

_____

_____

_____

_____

_____

_____

_____

_____

_____

_____

_____

_____

_____

_____

NOTES

Section 4

DIRECTING

Strategy 10:

Build a Winning Team

If you're searching for a style of management that will suit your employees as well as yourself, this chapter is the right place to look.

But first, let's review once popular, though ineffective, management philosophies that led to the formation of this management style which I later will detail.

If you're forty or older and have chalked up almost two decades of a sales career, you probably earned your first wages under the old "tell" style of management. This is the style in which a manager orders a salesperson to do something; when the salesperson raises a question, the manager tells the salesperson to forget the questions and follow the order; if the salesperson continues to object, he or she very well may object himself or herself right out of a job.

Such was the "tell" style of management. Organizations that subscribed to such management styles honestly earned the titles of "sweat shops," because the salespeople were to "work or else," and "body shops" because turnover was continually high. Salespeople were always going in and out of the organizations so rapidly that most of the offices should have installed revolving doors.

I don't think it takes a historian to prove that people have never liked being pushed around. But in the sales industry, the "tell" style of management faded during the late 1960's and early 1970's, when individualism was stressed and "do your own thing" and "fight the establishment" became catch phrase slogans for potential mavericks all across the country.

Consequently, many "telling" sales organizations were forced to change management strategies, lest they lose all competent and able salespeople. The field of sales is vast, and sales managers finally discovered that only the weak salespeople were retained under a dictatorship.

PHILOSOPHIES CHANGED

So many of these sales managers shifted their philosophies from the unacceptable form of "telling" to the equally unacceptable management style of asking, showing, hoping and, if all else failed, begging. All of a sudden, during the mid-1970s, sales managers who had been accustomed to barking orders and commands suddenly were playing "nice guys," begging their subordinates to do their jobs.

When a manager has to resort to begging to motivate a salesperson to act, the transfer of power is complete. Undoubtedly, many sales organization owners, witnessing this style of management, probably scratched their heads in wonder, asking themselves, "Who is the boss here, anyway?"

Salespeople want and need good leadership. Like I said in chapter one, people will conform to the minimum of any standards you set. But if you offer salespeople the option whether or not to perform to your specifications, most of them will pass, because it's much easier to fail than succeed. Without proper guidance, I think it's very reasonable to estimate that most salespeople would fail.

Still, I occasionally talk with sales managers of commissioned salespeople who are afraid to abandon this ask-show-hope-beg method of management. Several actually have told me that, on the advice of their attorneys, they cannot issue orders to their salespeople because they are independent contractors.

I once felt that way. During my first years as a real estate sales agent during the late 1960's, I used to work for a man who subscribed to the "tell" style of management so rigidly and tenaciously that, had he been born in Germany instead of America, he probably would have achieved worldwide infamy instead of Adolph Hitler.

This man was so domineering and direct—not to mention seemingly heartless—that we called him Hitler's Brother (behind his back, of course; to his face, it was always H. B.).

This guy was tough, let me tell you. If we made mistakes, he'd actually call them to our attention in no uncertain terms; if our real estate listings had flaws detrimental to the financial interests of the company (and, of course, our commissions), he would actually circle them with a red pen and make us go back to the homeowner to renegotiate on previously negotiated points.

Talk about embarrassing! This man would make me so mad, he'd actually force me to make money. One day, I had enough of his orders.

"You can't order me around," I said. "I'm an independent contractor."

"Fine," he said. "Go contract somewhere else."

Reassessing my position, I decided I had spoken a bit hastily and decided that it would be in my best interests to come back down to earth. From then on, I never had any problems taking direction.

But H. B. was no villain. God love him, he was just teaching me how to be independent. In retrospect, I can see that clearly, although it was difficult at the time. I always thought he had it out for me.

LARGE HEART VS. NO HEART

I remember once I was troubled with heart palpitations. I consulted a doctor, who administered an electrocardiogram and diagnosed me as having an enlarged heart. The good doctor warned me about the possible consequences of the ailment and strongly advised that I had better cut back on my activity to prolong my life.

I told H. B. about it the next day. No more extremely long days or hard work for me, I told him, or the doctor said I might die.

H. B. looked at me squarely in the eye and said, "Floyd, find a new doctor. Get another opinion."

I did. And I'm fine. At least I've lived long enough to build successful careers as a real estate agent, manager, trainer and, ultimately, a prominent results-oriented real estate sales and management speaker. And, last time I checked, my heart was still working fine.

So if your attorney has advised you not to issue directives to your salespeople, take H. B.'s advice instead and find another attorney. Get another opinion.

DEVELOP A TEAM

Let me detail for you the most powerful method of management in terms of getting production and positive results. If you subscribe to it, your organization (and you, too, of course) will earn more money easier and faster than ever before.

If you want to manage your team of sales associates, use the team style of management. It's nothing more than the "tell" style of management, cleverly disguised as the "ask-show-hope-and-beg" style.

It's much easier to direct one team than it is to direct ten individuals. With team management, you can delegate more minor tasks. With team management, you'll have more solutions to your problems, because you employ the brainpower of your staff for identifying and solving problems. And ten heads are better than one!

You'll increase your staff's productivity by creating a synergy, or the cooperative action of separate agents to provide an effect greater than the combination of the actions resulting from these agents had they acted independently. (A synergy is where a concerted impact is greater than the sum of its individual elements).

Building a team involves more effort than just getting salespeople to like each other. A team is cooperation. All teams in any sports contests are motivated by one goal and one goal only. Ten people motivated by a common goal will outproduce ten people working toward individualistic goals.

If you would build a team, there are four guidelines to follow. Each of these factors must be present, or there will be no team; instead, you'll have a band of individualists seeking their own personal glories with little or no interest toward the solvency of the company. But with all four of these factors, this band of individualists can increase your company's productivity and still look out for their own interests. Everybody wins!

1. **Common cause.** If you want your ten-member team to generate thirty sales per month, it might be unrealistic to expect three sales from each salesperson. But it wouldn't be unrealistic to expect thirty sales from the team as a whole. When individuals are managed, they are motivated by their own desires. By establishing a common cause, you add an important factor—peer pressure.

2. **Minimum standards.** A team will be better motivated to function by setting minimum standards for them to follow. Team members will hustle with more energy if they know they'll be raked over the coals for not achieving a particular level of production.

3. **Competent people.** To accomplish a common cause, you've got to have competent people who are willing to prospect, make appointments, be good company representatives and, above all, good salespeople. This is a must.

4. **Individual commitment.** Each and every member of the team must be willing to act as a team player, to commit him or herself to acting in the best interests of the team. Of course, a competent individual can be motivated to do this by illustrating how acting in the team's best interests is, in fact, acting in that person's own best interests.

Sounds easy, doesn't it? It is. But, of course, there is more to it than that. After all, if this were all that were involved in the total process of building a team, the need for your services would end once the team was formed.

YOU'VE GOT TO MAINTAIN

As any football player will tell you, the coach is necessary not only to build the team but to maintain it. A manager is needed for the same reasons. Anything built can be destroyed, and I've learned this through painful, personal experience.

As a trainer and consultant, I attempted thirty-four times to build teams for organizations operating in the red. Each time, I went into the office and the production charts looked like EKG reports of perilously slow heartbeats—a long straight line with a blip here and a blip there . . .

Thirty-one of those thirty-four times, I was able to direct and motivate the team to increase its production by fifty percent (the three unsuccessful occasions were the results of my efforts being vetoed by office management). I accomplished this with the factors I just detailed for you—**common cause, minimum standards, competent people and individual commitment.**

But in twenty-nine of those thirty-one successful efforts, production reverted to its previous levels within two months, because I didn't teach the sales managers and/or business owners what I had done!

I won't repeat that mistake here. Instead, I'm going to give you a list of guidelines to follow for maintaining your team.

As humans, we all have flaws; we're going to make mistakes from time to time, and this goes for managers as well as team players. Whenever you take note that things aren't going as they should, the fault may be with certain team members. But it also may be with you.

When the situation is not normal, I suggest that before criticizing any salesperson or the team in general, you first review this ten-point checklist. This consists of policies you should follow every day. If you do, you'll find that your team members will stay with you longer and will work for you more diligently.

THE MANAGER'S MANUAL

1. **Always provide a common goal.** This is the first rule of building a team. There always must be a common

goal. A lapse of even a week or so can be detrimental to the results you might envision. A football team's offensive efforts would be wasted if there were no goal to pursue. The same is true with your sales force. Keep the goal, or the carrot-on-a-stick, if you will, dangling before the team.

2. **Always require high standards.** Have them clearly stated in the company manual. If your salespeople refuse to adhere to the standards, then you must do something about it, either through written warning, reprimand or dismissal. If a salesperson doesn't meet your standards and you don't take corrective action, then you, in effect, have lowered your standards in the eyes of the remaining team members.

3. **Never criticize your salespeople in public.** That's tantamount to a slap in the face. It's demeaning, degrading, and definitely demoralizing. The person you criticize in the presence of others definitely will lose respect for you and will genuinely—and justifiably—like you less.

4. **Always praise your salespeople in public.** Praise is definitely power; sound your praises, when appropriate, at sales rallies and other assemblies.

5. **Encourage your team members to communicate, and listen to them.** This is simply good human relations. If your team members believe their voices are valuable and their opinions are honored, they will stay with you longer and work harder while they're there.

6. **Build on the positives.** Always stress the positive aspects of the team; don't dwell on the negatives. As a trainer of more than two thousand, six hundred ''Sweathogs'' throughout North America, I was occasionally

asked by agents to spend some time teaching managers to refrain from putting them down. There is a time for criticism, but it should be kept to a minimum. Build on the positive aspects of the team, and many of the negative points should disappear. If your team members continually warrant severe criticism, despite your sincere efforts to reinforce them positively, then perhaps you should stop criticizing and find yourself another team.

7. **You are a leader, not a cheerleader.** Cheerleaders don't play; they just cheer. Managers are like coaches; they're part of the game because they direct. Be a good coach and direct your team in a positive fashion. Encourage them to be enthusiastic, neater and more positive, and explain to them how this will produce results. Encourage them to use any sales tools that the company provides, again for results, not because you or the company owner ordered them to use them.

8. **Always make clear your expectations and ultimatums.** In any relationship, be it salesperson-manager, husband-wife, friend-friend, the number one flaw—the reason that the relationship comes to pieces (if not to blows)—is because neither party ever detailed their expectations and ultimatums. If a couple—before marrying—would sit down and discuss each other's do's and don't's and elicit mutual promises not to violate each other's agreed-upon code, the divorce rate would be drastically reduced (and possibly the marriage rate, for that matter).

9. **Direct your salespeople's activity and inspect their results.** Salespeople are likely to do what you inspect, rather than what you expect. Don't offer direction if you won't offer inspection, and the same applies in reverse: Don't inspect if you don't direct. You have

no right to criticize anyone after an inspection if you didn't offer direction in the first place.

10. **You have a team, not a staff.** Refer to your sales force as a team, rather than a staff. A staff implies a group of people acting as assistants to a person of a higher position. A team implies a group of people associated together in the pursuit of a common cause. It seems like such a little thing at best, but it's the little things that will undo you in the end.

Many of these points may seem like little things at best. So let me ask you now, have you ever been bitten by an elephant? Of course you haven't, because (as my colleague, Joel Weldon, observes) elephants don't bite. If they did, you'd keep a healthy distance from such mammoth-sized choppers, because you know they could prove to be your undoing.

But you undoubtedly have been bitten by a mosquito or a gnat. Little things bite. Since you're not afraid of little things, you probably get bitten quite often by little things. If you've ever been bitten repeatedly by mosquitoes or gnats, you know the cumulative effect of such bites can be most uncomfortable, indeed.

So watch out for the little things. They'll bite you. You can stay on the lookout for both little and big potential problems by following this manager's manual.

THE SIGNIFICANCE OF TEAMWORK

History has proven to us how powerful a team can be, and I'm not talking about the history of the Super Bowl. Instead, I'm talking about the power of franchising, or a group of individuals working together under a common cause. Perhaps the best modern-day example of franchising started with Ray Kroc and the very first McDonald's restaurant. Most Americans have but to drive a very short distance to witness the growth and power that franchising fostered with this corporation.

Franchising is, in effect, teamwork. Look what Japan accomplished in just forty years—the four decades that followed the devastating bombing of Hiroshima and Nagasaki. Through cooperative efforts, the Japanese people have taken over the electronics industry, the steel industry and brought the American automobile industry to its knees.

But if you really want to talk power and growth, let's talk about the country's first franchise—the union of thirteen independent colonies to form the country itself, the United States of America. The U.S. Constitution was the beginning of this franchise, and look how much power it has attained and how much growth it has experienced in two centuries. Meanwhile, the thirteen original members of the franchise—not to mention the thirty-seven that have since joined—have fared quite well in the process, thank you.

Remember, your organization is a franchise. It consists of a company operated by officials who want to grow and prosper, and it's supported by salespeople who likewise want to grow and prosper. They are human beings with job descriptions identical in wording (and very similar in definition) to your own.

Treat them as valued team members, unless or until they threaten to stage a "civil war" of sorts. But if they give you their best, give them your best.

And then, watch everybody involved—including yourself—prosper and grow.

That's called teamwork!

IN A CAPSULE

1. The old "tell" style of management went out with the Dark Ages. Good salespeople won't allow themselves to be ordered about for long under a system of management that offers fear of job loss as a motivator.

2. The "ask, show, hope and beg" method of management that evolved during the 1960s also is ineffective. When management has to resort to begging to get a salesperson to act, the transfer of power is complete.

3. The team style of management is by far the best, because it's easier to direct one team than it is to direct several different individuals. But four factors must be present, or you'll have no team. These factors are **common cause, minimum standards, competent people and individual commitment.**

4. Sales managers must adopt ten philosophies to keep their teams operating smoothly and without conflict. The philosophies are:
    —Always provide a common goal.
    —Always require high standards.
    —Never criticize salespeople in public.
    —Always praise your salespeople in public.
    —Encourage your team members to communicate, and listen to them.
    —Build on the positives.
    —Be a leader, not a cheerleader.
    —Always make clear your expectations and ultimatums.
    —Direct your salespeople's activities and inspect their results.
    —Refer to your team as a team, not as staff.

List the most important points you have gained from the
preceding Strategy:

_____

_____

_____

_____

_____

_____

_____

_____

_____

_____

_____

_____

_____

_____

_____

_____

_____

Strategy 11:

Know How To Manage Personality Problems, One-on-One

No matter how strong a team you have, there are going to be times when the actions of a lone individual will cause you to take corrective steps. Individual problems can sometimes threaten the smooth and efficient operation of the team itself.

Have you ever had a problem with any of your salespeople? Unless this is your first day as a sales manager, the answer to that question undoubtedly is "yes." (If not, congratulations! But you still might read this chapter anyway, because you never know what tomorrow will bring.)

Did you ever have a problem with someone procrastinating about making a prospecting contact or closing a sale? No matter how many times you've talked to this person, he or she just hasn't made any improvement. Or perhaps you've been plagued with a loud-mouth character who seems to know everything about selling—and managing as well.

If you've been in the sales business for any length of time at all, you've probably had to deal with not only those two problem types, but many others as well. How many personality problems can there be? As many as there are personalities. But for practical purposes, common personality traits that cause problems can be lumped into ten different categories.

When giving lectures and staging sales seminars, I've identified these ten personality types in the form of ten different personalities. There's **Ron "The Rebel," "Know-It-All" Nellie, "Old-Time" Ollie, Walt "The Workhorse," "Procrastinating" Paul, "Personal Problem" Paula, Earl "The Engineer," Tom "The Time Stealer," "Nice" Neil and "Negative" Ned.**

We'll get to know each of these individuals in this chapter. Of course, if you're in charge of a team of salespeople, you've probably gotten to know many, if not all, of these individuals already. So aside from identifying these personality types, I'll also give you a method of solving the problems that they cause by telling you how to handle the problem personality itself.

Although these problem personalities are identified as men and women, the names are for identification purposes only. Of course, anyone with these problems could be male or female alike. Personality problems of all types know no gender. But these "people" each will be identified as a "he" or a "she," depending on their given gender. This labeling should be accepted for identification purposes only and should not be viewed as the product of a sexist thought process.

MEET RON "THE REBEL"

Let me tell you how to recognize Ron "The Rebel." First, he's generally an above-average producer. He may even be your top producer. In any event, he'll be a valued member of your organization.

So how does he get the nickname "The Rebel"? Primarily because he rebels against the company by fighting company-approved systems. But he doesn't necessarily openly oppose such systems. Instead of challenging them verbally, he'll simply refuse to implement them. He'll "do his own thing," even though you'd prefer that he didn't.

Ron generally doesn't like to be bothered with company functions, such as meetings and rallies. When he does attend, he normally arrives late, sits sideways in the back of the room, doesn't take notes and leaves frequently for coffee breaks.

At work, it doesn't matter if the company prefers that salespeople prospect in a particular manner. Ron will do it his own way. Fortunately for Ron (but unfortunately for you), his method works—for him. Why is that unfortunate for you? Because Ron's method works only for him. It won't necessarily work for other team members who may admire Ron for his high production level and consequently may try to pattern their styles after him.

Therefore, Ron can be a problem. Since a certain percentage of the staff is likely to be influenced by him, the result could be crippling to your cause. Such a result might include the erosion of your authority (you'd eventually have three or four people showing up late, or not at all, for company meetings), not to mention the diminishing of the effectiveness of some of your team members (since Ron's systems won't necessarily work for them) and the dissolution of the teamwork structure you've tried to create. After all, if everyone is doing his or her "own thing," there isn't much room for teamwork.

So how do you handle Ron? You don't fire him, to say the least. After all, he's one of your best producers, if not your very best. Aside from this one small, but significant, problem, he otherwise fits into the team quite well.

Correct the problem that Ron causes by appealing to his senses of challenge and cooperation. In privacy, challenge Ron to implement and adhere to company systems. Or ask for a "personal favor." For example:

> "Ron, I need you to do me a personal favor. Everybody else on the team is going to follow this company-approved prospecting system. I know you don't need it, but I do want you to work with it just the same, because a lot of the other team members will follow your example. They need this new system, because your way just won't work for them. In fact, I'll bet you a dinner that you can't do me a favor by implementing this system. What do you say?"

If Ron is any kind of regular fellow at all, he'll comply with the manager's requests. Ron doesn't like to take orders, but the manager didn't give an order. Instead, the manager made a friendly bet that Ron couldn't do a favor for him. The manager appealed to Ron's sense of cooperation.

So when dealing with Ron "The Rebel," remember these two "key solutions"—"Bet you can't" and "Do me a favor."

 MEET "KNOW-IT-ALL" NELLIE

You can't help but recognize "Know-It-All" Nellie. She'll be the one who will know everything and won't mind telling you all about it. She's like Ron "The Rebel" in that she fights company systems. But unlike Ron, she doesn't fight quietly. She criticizes company policies openly during sales meetings and rallies. She must have the last word in any discussion.

Of course, Nellie isn't motivated by a cause as much as she yearns to be a respected individualist. For that reason, she often takes a stance in a meeting that is directly opposite from those taken by her peers, and she always does so in a boisterous manner. If a new product gains the approval of a majority of your team, Nellie will be against it. On the other hand, if the majority isn't very enthused about a new product, Nellie will find ways to defend it— passionately, of course.

Although her saving grace is the fact that she generally is an average to above-average producer, the fact remains that her ''know-it-all'' attitude threatens your teamwork structure, your authority and company image. And the reason for this is the fact that Nellie, aside from knowing it all, can be very negative at times. This explains her willingness to take issue with the majority.

And, of course, negativism is contagious. It can and will rub off on other salespeople, which can adversely affect the operations of the staff as a whole. If that happens, it won't take long for sales to plunge.

Nellie is just like most ''know-it-alls.'' They don't really think they know it all. If anything, they think they don't know enough. For this reason, or possibly another, they have lost (or never developed) confidence in themselves. They're insecure with something about themselves, and whatever it is must make quite a difference to them, because they're willing to be as obnoxious as possible in an attempt to conceal it.

As a manager, you can correct this problem fairly easily.

1. **Build Nellie's confidence by giving her authority.**

2. **Spend time in advance analyzing new ideas with Nellie.**

3. **Put Nellie in charge of program identification.**

The latter idea is really good when you're introducing a new company procedure. If you put Nellie in charge, not only will you eliminate your most vocal critic, but you'll also have a strong leader introducing your new procedure. With Nellie calling the shots, the rest of the team had better listen and get it right. Otherwise, they'll have to answer to her, and they won't like it!

Just remember, with "Know-It-All" Nellie, the key solutions are to give authority and feed her ego.

 ## MEET "OLD-TIME" OLLIE

He's one of the oldest (if not *the* oldest) member of the team, falling into the middle-age to senior citizen category. Fortunately for him, money isn't as important as it may have been when he was younger, because he's also one of the lowest (if not *the* lowest) producers. It's likely he was hired for his connections, or at least his perceived connections. Unfortunately for you, his connections are either non-productive or simply non-existent. His attitude is marked by a clear lack of enthusiasm. After all, he's got some age on him. He's seen it all before; there's no point in getting excited again. In fact, the only reason he's in the sales business at all is because his doctor told him to take it easy.

Like Nellie, Ollie destroys teamwork because he rejects what the majority accepts. He undermines your authority because he doesn't like to answer to anyone. He could ruin company image because he tends to ignore company policies and procedures in favor of his own "old-time" traditions. He also has a negative effect on team production, because he's a low producer.

As a result, his actions in general send a message to the rest of the team that it isn't important to be enthusiastic or to use company-approved sales technique presentations. His mere presence takes the fun out of teamwork and camaraderie because he is so indifferent to the sales environment.

About the only thing to do with Ollie is to try to get him to accept company procedures. Of course, if Ollie has been ignoring company procedures for years, he may have a lot of catching up to do. Your mission is to bring him up to date, one step at a time. You must "chip away" at Ollie's firm resolve to cling tenaciously to old customs. Get him to implement company systems, small portions at a time.

Remember, to solve Ollie's problems, you must "chip away" one item at a time. Don't expect him to change overnight. A little bit of change at a time should be sufficient. Sometimes, just getting him to attend one sales seminar or use one part of a visual presentation might lay a strong foundation for future positive development.

 MEET WALT "THE WORKHORSE"

Walt is a great guy. He's enthusiastic, a "rah-rah, go-get-'em" type whose production definitely qualifies for the peaks and valleys chart. He may set a record for sales over a thirty-day period, but all of his deals for the next three months will fall through because of errors he makes.

Walt's favorite word is "sure." No matter how many customers he may be required to contact in any given day, if someone asks him to work another into his schedule, he'll say, "Sure." He always wants to take on the world; of course, he rarely wins.

He's a bit on the sloppy side. His work often must be redone. Incomplete forms are not uncommon, his file folders have "dog ears" and his car usually is dirty. He may be working his eighth job within the past ten years, and in each of his jobs, he learned and performed well, temporarily.

Because Walt is the way he is, company image could suffer. Most of his work is done too quickly. Because he has so many other things to do, he often trims corners or forgets a task altogether. As a result, the client usually is disillusioned. Any document that Walt prepares for the client is usually an embarrassment for the company. Either it's unsightly, incomplete or outright erroneous.

The solution is simple: Walt must learn priority time management. He must understand that every minor detail doesn't necessarily have to be performed, at least immediately. He should learn to separate quality accomplishments from quantity work. Normally, a good way to help Walt is to direct his time management daily for about a month until good time practices become a habit with him. Enroll him in time management seminars, or assign him to give short lectures at sales meetings on the importance of time management.

Remember, Walt's problems can be reduced significantly, if not eliminated, by teaching him time management.

 # MEET "PROCRASTINATING" PAUL

Paul is a good individual. He always looks sharp, is a great talker and uses company systems. But he's still a below average producer, simply because he has a penchant for putting off the tasks that require nerve, such as contacting a prospect or closing a difficult sale.

His favorite words? "Not yet!" Whenever you ask him if he's made a particular contact or closed a particular deal, Paul is likely to respond by saying, "Not yet!"

Now Paul is not averse to work. He doesn't at all mind administrative, detailed or preparation work. But when it comes to doing what it takes to make money, he tends to postpone it.

The problem? Paul has a negative impact on sales production, because every customer that he doesn't contact and every sale he doesn't close is one less customer or sale for the company. He also presents a problem in team turnover, because Paul can represent as much as twenty-five to thirty percent of a sales team.

The solution: Teach Paul what he needs to know to succeed. This usually involves retraining him in the field. That's the only place he'll learn to do the things that take nerve in the sales business, such as cold-call prospecting and closing difficult sales.

Remember, "Procrastinating" Paul must be re-field trained to solve his problem.

 MEET "PERSONAL PROBLEM" PAULA

Like Walt "The Workhorse," Paula is a peaks-and-valleys producer whose average production tends to range just in the above-average category. If she could ever solve the scores of personal problems that plague her life, she probably could be a super saleswoman. Her behavior is consistent and pleasant. But she causes office problems by bringing her problems into the office.

She's what I call an "honest con." She's always using people, not so much to get ahead, but to get favors. She learned early in life that a halfway decent excuse and the right facial expression can prompt virtually anyone to do virtually anything for her, such as loan her a car or cover for her during her scheduled office time. Sometimes, Paula will even "con" clients into doing things that Paula herself should be doing for the clients.

The problem? Paula is destroying the company image, because customers may resent dealing with her. She also destroys the teamwork concept because she creates dissension among the team. Her co-workers get tired of covering for her or going out of their way to help her out. They also may resent any special treatment that Paula may get because of the demands on her schedule necessitated by her personal problems.

The solution? Give Paula a short-term ultimatum, informing her that the next time a personal problem surfaces that interferes with company productivity or a company function, she's either finished, fined or punished in some way. Also, you must remind her that any problems that do occur should be brought directly to management attention and should not be shared with other staff members.

Remember, to solve Paula's problem, give her a short-term ultimatum.

 ## MEET EARL "THE ENGINEER"

Earl is the fellow on your staff who is always getting started to get started, unless he's getting ready to get ready to get started. He usually has an analytical outlook on life, and possibly comes from an engineering, mathematical or science background.

Many times, Earl is in the sales business because he has been laid off from a previous job or is between jobs. He is attracted to sales by the lure of a good income and the attractiveness of a job that doesn't restrict a person to traditional daytime hours.

Earl will spend months analyzing the market area, meticulously compiling data on its demographics and client base. Everything he produces is a clean deal, put together properly from beginning to end.

So what's the problem? Earl is so busy analyzing and compiling data that he rarely produces. Even though his transactions are clean, they're few and far between. And when Earl does close a deal, he has a tendency to overservice. Many times, he offers a tremendous amount of service before the actual sale itself.

Earl's lack of production is costing the company. People like Earl usually contribute to a high rate of turnover within the company because of their lack of production.

The fault there lies with Earl's analytical personality. He believes

168

you shouldn't "talk somebody into something" unless you can irrefutably prove the outcome. He doesn't realize that salespeople can be effective without knowing every single fact and statistic concerning the product. He's very reluctant to make any claim to a client without knowing absolutely everything there is to know about the product. As a result, he seldom puts himself in face-to-face situations with clients.

Yet, Earl could be a superstar if you can teach him the balance between people knowledge and product knowledge. He must be taught sales psychology as well as product knowledge. You must prove to Earl that many sales are made by salespeople who don't disclose all the facts.

To put it simply, make Earl effective by teaching him the art of selling.

 MEET TOM "THE TIME-STEALER"

Everybody knows Tom. He's a gregarious fellow. He's very friendly with everyone within the company. A real socializer, he seldom does anything alone. That's where the problem lies. Tom usually is so busy socializing, he seldom has time to work. Therefore, his production is very sporadic; he is definitely a low producer. (Of course, Tom doesn't need much money, because his wife works, too.)

But that's not the extent of his problem. When you come into the office and see a group of people standing in a huddle, Tom will usually be in the center, cracking jokes or offering anecdotes about his personal experiences. When he goes to lunch, he not only takes more time than necessary, but he also takes along other salespeople, who also stay longer than necessary because they're having fun with Tom. As a result, Tom not only uses his time unwisely, but he encourages others to waste their time, also.

The problem? Tom adversely affects sales production—his own, plus that of others he encourages to waste time with him. His magnetic personality and bad time habits are a deadly combination to your team's production level. Even when Tom finally gets around to meeting a customer, he'll spend too much time making small talk, thus avoiding all the things he must do to make a sale.

The solution? Close daily direction. Tom is more apt to do what you inspect rather than what you expect. Fear is a great motivator with Tom. He's never been fired from a job, and he couldn't live with himself if he ever was discharged. So make sure you keep Tom extremely busy working with customers. If he knows you will be checking behind him, he won't be encouraged to "shoot the breeze" with anyone who will listen.

Remember, make a worker out of Tom by directing his activity daily.

 MEET "NICE" NEIL

"Nice" Neil is truly a wonderful fellow. He is extremely likeable. Customers and fellow salespeople alike think a lot of him. He's in the sales business because he enjoys work and people, too.

In a way, Neil is really quite an asset to your sales team. His sunny disposition, cheerful manner and neat appearance serves to enhance the spirit of teamwork, your authority and company image, the latter of which is further boosted by his usually active role in church and civic affairs. There's no destructive intent on his part; such is not Neil's nature. He is also most helpful by volunteering (if not actually taking it upon himself) to do non-revenue producing tasks such as low priority clerical and clean-up tasks, as well as making coffee for the team.

So what's the problem with Neil? He is so nice that he thinks the art of selling borders on bad taste. He has an extreme distaste for pushy people and will take every step imaginable to avoid ever being described as such. Neil truly desires to be nice. In fact, he is so nice that he will not sell anything for fear of possibly offending someone.

For that reason, he's an extremely low producer. But Neil won't starve, because he usually doesn't need money. He's either independently wealthy or has a spouse who works and earns a good income. That's why he can afford to be so nice, because he doesn't usually need money. Work to him is an escape. He enjoys it because it's a happy alternative to staying at home alone, watching soap operas.

How do you correct Neil's problem? You don't. Only Neil can do that, and usually, this won't happen unless something drastic occurs in his life. If the source of his outside support were to dry up suddenly, Neil might decide that he couldn't afford to be so nice anymore. But as long as that doesn't happen, he's likely to remain the same, "Nice" Neil.

So if you can't correct his problem, you might as well take advantage of it. Let him do the work that he enjoys best—tasks that preserve the concepts of teamwork, your authority and company image. (Where else can you find free clerical and janitorial help? And if it makes Neil happy, why not?)

The solution for Neil is to give him non-selling assignments. Don't count on his production, ever! And don't give him leads, because his touch will turn them from potential gold into dust.

Remember, to make the best of "Nice" Neil, delegate small tasks to him.

 ## MEET "NEGATIVE" NED

I hope you don't have a "Negative" Ned on your team. But even if you don't, odds are that you eventually will recruit one by mistake.

Ned can't see the positive side to anything. He's usually whining and complaining. His favorite words are "Yes, but . . ." And he'll use them whenever you have anything generally nice or encouraging to say to him. For example, you might say, "I'll expect you to have a good month, Ned," to which he'll reply, "Yes, but the economy is bad and . . ." Or, "Isn't this an exciting new product we're selling?" to which Ned will reply, "Yes, but I don't like it because it costs too much . . ."

Ned is the type of person whom, if you're honest with yourself, you don't care to have around you, simply because he is too negative. His attitude will pull down your positive attitude and those of the other team members. For that reason, he is a threat to the concept of teamwork. And he definitely has a severely adverse impact on sales production because of his own lack of production.

So how do you solve the problem? Unfortunately, you don't. The problem probably started when he was two years old. He simply can't be managed out of it. The longer he remains on the team, the more of a drain to everyone else he will be, because negativism, unfortunately, is very contagious.

The solution: Fire him. That's all. There's nothing else you can do, except to try your best not to hire him in the first place.

SEVEN-STEP METHOD
FOR PROBLEM SOLVING

Now that you're acquainted with these problem personalities, I want to give you an effective process for confronting salespeople with these problems and for working with them to reach satisfactory resolutions to their problems.

But first, let me caution you. Using this plan does not mean that the person will be perfect forever. It also doesn't mean that another personality problem won't surface later. In fact, some people have more than one of these personality problems. When one goes away, another surfaces. For example, Tom "The Time Stealer" could easily become a "Procrastinating" Paul or, if his problem is truly solved, a Ron "The Rebel."

But this plan I'm going to teach you works, judging by numerous sales managers to whom I've taught it over my career as a real estate manager, trainer and speaker. In fact, a sales manager in Atlanta told me recently that she used this process on three of her salespeople, and the results were fantastic.

I'm also not saying that this process is foolproof. Quite the contrary. Some people just won't change, like "Nice" Neil and "Negative" Ned. But if a person is able to change himself or herself, this seven-step process is a fine catalyst to bring about a change for the better.

Step One: "Is He/She Worth It?"

Step one is simple. Answer either "yes" or "no" to the question, "Is he/she worth it?" Is the salesperson under fire worth your time and effort to help bring about an improvement? For example, if the salesperson has intentionally done something dishonest, then the answer should be "no," and you should fire the salesperson. Or, if you've already talked to this person more times than you care to remember about the problem, and there has been no improvement, then the answer again should be "no," and you should fire at will.

Otherwise, consider the following: You only have three choices of avenues to take if you choose not to fire the person outright.

Your first option is, you can merely hope the problem will go away. The truth of the matter is, unless something drastic occurs in the problem salesperson's life, the odds are slim to none that the individual will change without some assistance.

Your second option is, you can merely live with the problem.

But unless you have an upside-down organizational chart, you are in charge of your sales team. If there's a problem on your team that's costing your company money, you should do something about it or make room for a sales manager who will take corrective action. After all, keeping the team operating smoothly and efficiently is the sales manager's job.

Your third option is to use this plan. So if you've determined that the salesperson is indeed worth your time and effort to correct the problem, then proceed to step two.

Step Two: Have a "Special" Meeting

Step two is to meet at an unusual time and place. This is called "impact communication." Staging a conference with the salesperson at your office during the regular workday won't deliver nearly the impact that a face-to-face talk will carry if it's conducted before or after working hours at a place other than the office.

If the problem salesperson is one of your better producers, perhaps you might stage the meeting over a nice dinner at a local restaurant. If he or she is one of your lower producers, you might have the salesperson stop by your house and meet in your recreation room over a cup of coffee. In any event, the salesperson's thought process is likely to begin solving the problem while he or she is en route to the special meeting, simply because the meeting obviously, by its time and location, is special.

Step Three: Point Out the "Good Things"

Praise the salesperson for his or her good qualities. If the salesperson is worth your time and effort to correct the problem, that's a good indication that there is much about the salesperson that is positive and productive. Call this to the salesperson's attention, and praise him or her for it. Perhaps this valued quality might be the salesperson's persistence, determination, high energy, personality or neat appearance. Or the valued quality might be a particular transaction that the salesperson put together. Spend some time communicating to the person what you like about him or her. This is essential, because it will put the salesperson in a more conducive frame of mind to accept the criticism that will follow.

Step Four: Straight-Line the Problem

Communicate the problem to the salesperson with the least possible waste of words. Don't beat around the bush. Get right to the point. You can be tactful, but still stick to the point. For example, "So, Charlie, those are the things I like about you. But you've been putting off doing the things necessary to make money in this business, and it's got to stop right now, or something drastic will have to be done. Did you hear what I said?"

Step Five: Exchange Points of View

Get the salesperson to see the problem from your point of view. It's important that you illustrate to the salesperson how his or her problem adversely affects the company, not necessarily the salesperson. Until you can get the salesperson to see the problem from your point of view, the odds of eliminating the problem will be slim.

So take your time and build a good case. Have statistics, proof and analogies to prove your point. Show how the problem is costing the company, not the salesperson. Remember, for many people, money (past a certain point) isn't a great motivator. Unless you show how the problem is hurting the company, the salesperson probably won't be motivated to change his or her behavior.

Step Six: Discuss the Solution

The two of you should be able to arrive at some type of viable, mutually agreeable solution. Talk it out, and reach an agreement.

Step Seven: Agree in Writing to a Solution

Agree in writing to a solution, a plan of action and the ultimatum for not solving the problem. Make sure the document is signed by both you and the salesperson, and give a copy to the salesperson. Once the salesperson has a copy of the agreement in hand, the odds of correcting the problem greatly increase.

Again, this plan isn't foolproof. It's no miracle cure; that is, don't expect a salesperson with a penchant for procrastination not to slip into his or her old routine from time to time. But if a salesperson has it within himself or herself to make a marked change for the better, this plan can be the catalyst to bring about the change.

IN A CAPSULE

1. Ron "The Rebel" is an above-average producer who fights company systems by refusing to implement them. This tends to erode your authority and threatens the concept of teamwork. Solve the problem by appealing to his sense of cooperation. Privately challenge him to adhere to company systems. Ask him to do it as a personal favor for the good of the team.

2. "Know-It-All" Nellie is an average to above-average producer who openly fights company systems. Her sometimes negative attitude threatens the teamwork concept and company image. Solve the problem by building her confidence. Give her authority, review new ideas with her and put her in charge of implementing new programs.

3. "Old-Time" Ollie is a middle-aged to elderly low producer whose lack of enthusiasm and unwillingness to adhere to company systems can threaten your authority, company image, sales production and the concept of teamwork. "Chip away" at his firm resolve to adhere to his old-time customs by teaching him one new procedure at a time.

4. Walt "The Workhorse" is an enthusiastic, peaks-and-valleys producer whose work tends to be sloppy. This can adversely affect company image. Teach Walt how to better manage his time.

5. "Procrastinating" Paul is a below-average producer who threatens company production because of his penchant for postponing actions that would lead to a sale. Solve his problem by taking him back out in the field for more training.

6. "Personal Problem" Paula is a slightly above-average producer who just can't keep personal problems out of the office. This causes dissension among the team members, who often must go out of their way to accommodate Paula as she deals with her latest life crisis. Give her a short-term ultimatum.

7. Earl "The Engineer" is a slow starter whose unwillingness to persuade a prospect to buy is adversely affecting your team's production level. Teach Earl the art of selling.

8. Tom "The Time-Stealer" is a low producer who places more importance on socializing than selling. Offer close daily direction, and inspect his work daily.

9. "Nice" Neil is an extremely likable fellow, but he's also a low producer who has an extreme distaste for selling because he doesn't want to offend anyone. But he is indeed an asset to the company, since his agreeable manner and neat appearance actually enhances the concept of teamwork, your authority and company image. Take advantage of Neil's aversion to sales by assigning him to perform non-selling tasks.

10. "Negative" Ned is a chronic, irreformable whiner and complainer who can't or won't see the positive side to anything. His negative attitude destroys the concept of teamwork and sales production, because negativism is contagious. Fire him.

11. Correct these personality problems with a seven-step process. Step one, is the person worth the time and effort? If so, proceed to step two, which is to stage a meeting with the salesperson at an unusual time and place. Then point out the salesperson's good qualities, straight-line the problem, get the salesperson to see the problem from your point of view, discuss the solution and agree in writing.

178

List the most important points you have gained from the
preceding Strategy:

_____

_____

_____

_____

_____

_____

_____

_____

_____

_____

_____

_____

_____

_____

_____

NOTES

Section 5

MOTIVATING

Strategy 12:

Only Have Contests that Work!

Not too long ago in the context of geology and history, I had a revelation that hit me like a ton of bricks. The force of its impact was tantamount to a religious experience. It was almost as if the Hand of God reached down from the heavens and tapped me on the shoulder, while a rich, deep voice said, "Wickman, you've just figured out the secret to increasing sales production."

I don't mean to be sacrilegious or sanctimonious, because I'm certain that this discovery in itself will have no bearing on whether or not I get into heaven when I'm through with the sales business. Instead, I want to impress upon you that there is no better way to increase your sales team's production than by staging contests.

When conducting seminars, I always write the word "contests" and quickly add an asterisk beside it, because just the word "contests" doesn't tell the whole story. I've seen some great contests bomb because all the ingredients weren't there.

For example, I've seen some companies making X amount of

dollars announce a contest and, by the end of the contest, the company was making X minus Y dollars, and the winners still got rewarded.

That shouldn't happen. Sure, contests are great for motivating salespeople to increase their production, but the main reason behind the contest—the only reason as far as the sales manager is concerned—is to help the company make more money. If that isn't accomplished, the contest effort has been wasted.

Remember H. B. (Hitler's Brother), my old boss? Here are his words on the subject: "Wickman, the only reason we have contests is to make more money—as a result of the contests—than we were making before. We don't do anything if it won't get results."

We've already established the fact that money, alone, isn't a motivator. But when you combine money or some other valued award (such as a vacation or some other benefit to the salesperson) with a little friendly competition, you've got a powerful motivational tool that won't cost you a cent and should channel a greater flow of dollars into your organization.

But don't get contests confused with incentives. Contests are short-range boosters of income, which can last from one hour to a maximum of thirty days (a longer period of time is not advised because it's easy for team enthusiasm to wane after a month.) Incentives, on the other hand, are rewards for salespeoples' long-range accomplishments, such as setting new individual sales records.

First, let's establish the four types of contests, ranking them in order of ascending effectiveness:

1. **Individual contest.** With a ten-member sales team, the top three producers get prizes, and the other seven get nothing. This is the least effective contest, because the sales team already knows who will win when the contest is announced.

   Never have individual winners; first, this concept doesn't earn the company any extra money, because seven of your team members won't be motivated to make an extra effort, and second, because individual contests shatter the team concept you've labored so long to create. Incentives should be offered to top producers for long-term accomplishment. That's the way to reward your most valued individual team members. But contests should be staged to reward the team as a whole.

2. **Team Vs. Team Within An Office.** If you have more than fifteen people on your team, split the team into two groups and pit one against the other. Appoint a member of each group to serve as the group leader, who would be responsible for assisting in training, motivating, recruiting, directing and upgrading. You'll be relieved of a lot of work, and you'll have a lot more energy in your office. Although this concept is far more effective than the individual contest, it still wouldn't be my first choice of a contest, because why split a team if it's not necessary?

3. **Challenge another office.** A little friendly competition between rivals can be a great motivator. Although only one team can win, both companies will benefit if the net result is increased production. Another office under the same franchise would be a great target for a challenge.

4. **Team Vs. The Boss.** This is a great contest between contests. With this concept, you can always have a contest in progress. Contests can last as long as thirty days, or as little as an hour. The payoff can be as simple as beer and pizza. The payoff can be simple embarrassment; if the team members meet the boss's challenge, the boss may commit himself or herself to attend the next board meeting clad in a tutu. If you have any team members who don't like you, the thought of embarrassing you might motivate them to expend a little extra effort. It's a great motivator.

Those are the four types of contests that can motivate your sales team to strive for greater production. But just because I describe four kinds of cakes doesn't tell you how to go about making them. All cakes and contests have ingredients which must be included if the end result is to be worth the effort. If you make a cake and neglect to add eggs or milk, chances are good the cake won't turn out to be what you expected.

So let me offer you a contest flow chart containing fifteen ingredients that will make your contest most successful.

1. **KISS—Keep it simple, sales manager.** I've seen contests that only mathemeticians and engineers could figure out exactly what it would take to win. I've sat at the head tables of rallies for different franchise organizations and heard contests being kicked-off with details that would confuse wizards. The manager would announce the contest by saying that each salesperson would get eighty-three points per sale per first price category, one hundred six points per second price category sale, one hundred ninety points per third price category, etc. The expressions on the salespeople's faces were not the type you should want to see when announcing a contest. It's hard to be enthusiastic if you don't understand the components of the contest. Keep it simple. One point per accomplishment keeps the rules fair. The more rules you have, the less fair it is. Simple scoring maintains the fairness of a contest.

2. **Only reward the "do's."** There is a limit to the things that salespeople can "do." For example, a salesperson can "do" an appointment, a lead or a sale, because the salesperson is in a controlled situation. But a salesperson can't "do" dollar volume. If you kick off your contest with dollar volume as criteria for winning points,

you will be asking your salespeople to work for something over which they have no control. It takes just as much skill, effort and determination (if not actually more) to put together a transaction involving "X" amount of dollars as it does one involving "X" times five. Salespeople have no control over dollar volume.

3. **Always have a collective objective.** Give every member of your team a common purpose. If the contest is "beat the boss," then every team member must "beat the boss." Instead of making each person in a ten-member staff come up with three sales to beat the boss, it would be better to require the entire team to produce thirty sales. This makes it a team effort. It doesn't matter to you how the team beats the boss, provided that the overall goal is met. If your top five producers pull in six sales each, the bottom five producers could do absolutely nothing, and the team still would "beat the boss."

4. **Kick off with pizzazz.** If the contest is worth staging at all, it's worth announcing with enthusiasm. I've seen some contests announced that sounded like cancer was coming to town. Build enthusiasm on your team by announcing your contest visually (posters) as well as verbally.

5. **Have silly fun.** If there is one thing I've learned in the sales business, it's the fact that we're all tall kids. People of all ages like to have fun, and the best work is accomplished when the workers are having a ball. Contests lend themselves quite well to the concept of having fun while you work. But your salespeople won't feel comfortable having fun unless you take the lead.

6. **Include a follow-up system.** Keep track of team members' progress, and you'll keep the contest alive. If

189

you don't follow-up, the enthusiasm may wane, if the contest doesn't actually die itself. My old boss, H. B., found a way to keep the contest alive by sending weekly reports of our standing in the contest to our spouses. Coming home tired and having to explain to the spouse why your name was on the bottom of the performance list was not a fun thing to do.

7. **Set a reward for winning.** Otherwise, where is the incentive to compete? A hearty handclasp and a few words of praise isn't enough. Of course, the best rewards are those that go to each team member.

8. **Set a penalty for losing.** This can be an added motivation for winning, because losing can be sufficiently unpleasant. For example, if you challenge your team to make X number of sales per week, you might reward them by taking them out to dinner plus wearing any hat they would like for you to wear while in the restaurant. One has only to go to K mart to see how many ridiculous hats are on the market. But if the team fails to meet the contest requirement, then they take you to dinner, plus they'll wear the hats that you bring. I've had experiences with my Sweat Hogs who earned an extra several thousand dollars because they didn't intend to wear my hats. Let me tell you something, I'm known for my hats (you'll never see me wear them, unless I lose a bet).

9. **Broadcast the contest.** Let all of your franchise people know about it. Peer pressure pays off.

10. **Post a progress chart.** Keep track of each individual's accomplishments on a chart posted for all to see. And, of course, include a column for overall team standing, because that's what ultimately counts. But the individual

190

listings can be great incentives to the low producers and good ego gratification to the hard workers.

11. **Stick to your pay-off date.** If and when your team wins the contest, keep your word and pay-off according to plan. If you don't, the next time you want to stage a contest, you may find that no one will want to play.

12. **Challenge your team into the contest, don't announce.** There are two ways to offer news of a contest. You could simply announce the contest and its rules and ask for questions. But a better way would be to present the contest idea to your team members, but leave entirely to them the decision as to whether a contest will actually be staged. Or, you might tease your team members by asking a teasing question, such as, "How would you like to have dinner without any work on your part?" Then, drop the subject for a while, then return to it. "About dinner now, how many of you really have nerve?" Of course, your team members will wonder what your point is, but again, you drop the subject. After a few moments, then you might challenge your team members by saying, "I was going to make a deal with you. If you make so many sales, I'd buy you dinner." When you finally present the idea, it will be met with anticipation by your sales team.

13. **Build the foe.** If the boss is the "enemy," so to speak, build him or her up as the foe. When I was a sales manager, I would make posters with my pictures on them, usually adding an inflammatory caption, such as, "You can't beat the boss." And, of course, I'd be giving a sly grin in the pictures. One guy made a statement of his own by drawing a noose on the poster around my neck. Of course, it's all silly fun, and that's what you want.

14. **Get individual commitment.** Make sure that each and every member of your sales team is willing to engage in the contest. This is important to build team spirit. Of course, there always may be a lone, stick-in-the-mud holdout, but peer pressure from the other members of the group can provide sufficient persuasion. You might even leave the room while your team members are deciding to allow for freer exchange of conversation.

15. **Pay off with pizzazz.** If your team wins the contest, give them a prize worth winning. Have fun when you take them to dinner; most restaurants will allow you to have fun, provided it's in good taste and doesn't involve the police, motorcycle gangs or destruction of property. If you've split the team, the winners can eat steak with all the trimmings, while the losers eat beans out of paper plates and wear silly hats.

If your contest includes all of these points, it would take virtually a depression for the company not to benefit with greater sales. Of course, that's the real reason for staging a contest. Salespeople may become more motivated, may be inspired by their increased production and may, as a result, become better salespeople in general. And that's good. But that's not the main purpose of the contest.

Don't stage a contest unless you want to make more money. If you stage a contest for reasons other than that, you'll lack the necessary enthusiasm to charge your team members. It will be of secondary importance to you, and your team members will pick up on this. If it's not important to you, it won't be important to them.

CONTEST FLOW CHART

Ingredient   **Method**

1. KISS – Keep it simple, sales
   manager.   _____

                                               _____

2. Only reward the "do's"   _____

                                               _____

3. Always have a collective
   objective   _____

                                               _____

4. Kick off with pizzazz   _____

                                               _____

5. Have silly fun   _____

                                               _____

6. Include a follow-up system   _____

                                               _____

7. Set a reward for winning   _____

                                               _____

8. Set a penalty for losing   _____

                                               _____

CONTEST FLOW CHART (cont.)

Ingredient	Method
9. Broadcast the contest	_____ _____
10. Post a progress chart	_____ _____
11. Stick to your pay-off date	_____ _____
12. Challenge your team into the contest, don't announce	_____ _____
13. Build the foe	_____ _____
14. Get individual commitment	_____ _____
15. Pay off with pizzazz	_____ _____

Note: Use this flow chart each time you have a contest.

IN A CAPSULE

1. Contests are the best way to motivate salespeople, but the contest must include all the ingredients.

2. The main purpose behind staging a contest should be to make more money for the company. If this doesn't happen, the effort has been wasted.

3. Contests are short-range boosters of income, which can last from one hour to a maximum of thirty days (a longer period of time is not advised because it's easy for team enthusiasm to wane after a month.) Incentives, on the other hand, are rewarding people for long-range accomplishments, such as setting new individual sales records.

4. There are four types of contests—individual competition, team versus team within an office, office versus office and team versus boss. The individual competition is usually not a good idea, because everyone will know from the start that the top producers will win. Team versus team within an office can be good, but why split a team if it's not necessary? Office versus office is great for friendly competition, and team versus boss is a great contest between contests.

5. The fifteen ingredients of a successful contest are to keep it simple, only reward the "do's," always have a collective objective, kick off with pizzazz, have silly fun, include a follow-up system, set a reward for winning, set a penalty for losing, broadcast the contest, post a progress chart, stick to your pay-off date, challenge your team, build the foe, get individual commitment and pay off with pizzazz.

List the most important points you have gained from the
preceding Strategy:

_____

_____

_____

_____

_____

_____

_____

_____

_____

_____

_____

_____

_____

_____

_____

_____

_____

NOTES

Section 6

UPGRADING

Strategy 13:

Use the Six Steps to Success

What would you do with an automobile that stopped working? Would you junk it? Only if the vehicle's state of disorder was beyond repair.

Otherwise, you would, most likely, take the vehicle to a mechanic, who would diagnose the problem and make the necessary repairs. Perhaps a clog in the fuel line or a loose fan belt is causing the problem, which can be corrected with a minimum of difficulty.

On the other hand, the malfunction could be more serious. Perhaps the radiator is riddled with leaks, or the carburetor is on its last go-around, doomed to expire long before your current license tag. In such cases, the car could still be repaired with major effort and expense.

But repair is possible. You wouldn't junk the car unless the mechanic assured you that the expense involved in repair would outweigh the value of the car. Yet, if repair was warranted but you continued to drive the car, eventually the vehicle might very well be junked. Prolonged faulty operation can prove extremely detrimental to any machine.

Prolonged faulty operation of a sales team can be detrimental to its effectiveness, too. When your sales team stops working properly, for whatever reason, be it a faulty economy, too many underqualified team members or spring fever, it might be premature to fire the whole bunch. Besides, such effort would be too costly in terms of time and expense. Other upgrading steps may be more prudent.

To upgrade a sales organization means to enhance it, and there are several ways to go about this:

—**Set larger goals.** If the organization sold X number of goods, services or products last year, it might project the current year's dollar volume at X plus Y. In this case, the sales organization would be upgraded by establishing a new objective.

—**Personal improvement.** The manager may decide to get the staff involved in a personal and professional development program and/or other training directly related to their positions.

—**Fire.** When a sales organization is in a rut or actually digressing, upgrading of the organization is imperative. A sales manager might discharge the bottom producer or producers to eliminate the deadwood and make room for newer, and hopefully more competent, salespeople. This process is analogous to what might happen to a dying plant. Rather than trying to talk it back to life or drowning it with water, it might be better to clip off the dead branches for the benefit of the plant as a whole. If this isn't done, the entire plant could die. Firing a salesperson for lack of production also sends a strong message to other associates that weak, nonproductive salespeople won't survive.

Firing should be a last resort method only, obviously. But if there are members of your team whose trends of poor productions seem irreversible, it might be to your advantage to eliminate the problem people and concentrate on rebuilding the team.

As a manager, your sales team is your vehicle to success. It will serve you no better or no worse than the attention you devote to it. When production problems that threaten to impact adversely on company profits develop, it will be your job to identify the problems and correct them.

SIX STEPS TO SUCCESS

When serious problems arise, you can combat them with a six-step process designed to increase production and, ultimately, profits. But first, a word of warning. Never use this six-step weapon unless it is absolutely imperative. This is the secret weapon that should only be used under extenuating circumstances. If you use it when times are good, the damage to office morale can turn those good times into bad ones, indeed.

Instead, this plan should be used only when times are bad and in dire need of improvement. Then, the action will be perceived by your sales team members (most of them, anyway) as necessary and positive to improve the company's financial situation.

There are three times that I recommend that you use this six-step plan for survival (or improvement, whichever word suits your situation and/or fancy). Use it when you want to:

—**Increase productivity.** The plan will prove beneficial to elevate the company's financial status from survival to profit, from profit to securing a market share, from securing a market share to capturing a greater market share.

—**Reorganize.** The plan will be a good vehicle for making a major change within your sales organization. It would be appropriate to kick-off the reorganization with the six-step formula.

—**Build a team from the ashes of ruin.** If all else fails in trying to unite those ten or so individuals on your sales force, this plan should do the trick.

STEP 1:
PEOPLE ANALYZER

Teams are made up of people. Most problems that arise within sales organizations are people problems, not technical problems. Consequently, when it's necessary to enhance or increase, we must get more production out of the people.

So take an aerial view of your sales force. Out of ten people or so, you're bound to be very fond of some of them and indifferent, if not outright resentful, of others. But it's important that you put your personal feelings aside and look at each one of them in terms of how they relate to the majority of the force.

I suggest that you list each team member's name along with your own on a sheet of paper (See Diagram on page 209.) Then, at the top of the page, make four category headings, with the columns to extend vertically down the page. The categories will be:

—**Current perceived attitude.**

—**Noticeable effort.**

—Current relative production.

—Consistent use of company approved systems.

After this is done, then rate each sales associate, and yourself, on a plus or minus basis.

For example, suppose sales associate A has a good attitude and works diligently to pull his weight. Yet, his production is below par, and his use of company approved sales systems is haphazard at best. Rate this salesperson a plus on attitude and effort, but give him a minus on production and systems.

Forget about any personal feelings you may have while using this rating system. This is important, because to the degree that you use the system seriously, you'll increase your sales force productivity accordingly.

By all means, don't let a person's good potential influence your assessments. You'll take note that none of the four columns deals with potential, and there's a good reason for that.

No matter how much a person may have going for him or her, it won't make one iota of difference in terms of that person's production, unless the person is willing to convert the potential into power. Or, to put it simply, potential doesn't count! It doesn't take any potential whatsoever to work, or to have a good attitude. If you use this system, you must remain as objective as possible.

It's important that you also are honest about yourself because, and I know this may hurt, you could be part of the problem. Perhaps your attitude might not be what it should be, or your efforts may be below standard. Even sales managers have their rough times; after all, they're salespeople, too. They're selling the positive benefits of work to their sales teams, and if, for any reason, the team doesn't appear to be buying, it can get them down. That's only normal!

But to reverse a slump in production, it is imperative that you first make sure you're not part of the problem. If you are, it's doubly imperative to clean up your own act before critiquing those who would look to you for direction and, possibly, might even use you as a role model.

Makes you feel quite important, doesn't it? It might even sound a little scary. But it's true. So give yourself an honest review, and if you rate any minuses, change them into pluses before you go to work on your subordinates.

The people analyzer is a powerful tool that, a clear majority of the time, will support your natural instincts. It will help you identify major problems within the sales team. When you identify the problem person or people, you have two options. Either use the seven-step process for improvement or go to step two.

STEP 2: FIRE

If the problem person has all the positive qualities of "Negative" Ned, you may want to get rid of him or her right away. Firing may well be the hardest step of all of this six-step process, so be thankful that you get it behind you toward the beginning of the process.

Now you wouldn't fire each and every person with a minus. If you did that, you'd have to fire most of the team and yourself, too. But when there are real problems with people who seem, at least for the foreseeable future, to be irreformable, you should fire yourself if you don't fire them, because you certainly aren't doing yourself or the company any favors.

Firing is the most visually effective way of communicating a standards message to the other members of your sales team. If a salesperson's production falls below standard, don't give him or her the chance to resign; allowing a person to resign because of poor production does not send a very good message to the sales force's survivors.

PEOPLE ANALYZER

List the name of all persons in office regardless of position	Current Perceived ATTITUDE	Noticeable EFFORT	Current Relative PRODUCTION	Consistent Use of Company APPROVED SYSTEMS

I once was hired as a consultant for a sales firm in Newark, New Jersey and was picked up at the airport by the office manager. On the way to the office, I conducted a people analyzer on the manager's staff, and I rated pluses and minuses in accordance with the manager's assessments, which she gave me as she drove toward Newark.

Before we ever got to Newark, I had already determined the manager's problem—a woman named Julie who had rated four minuses on the people analyzer.

"Cathy," I said to the manager. "You've got to fire Julie."

Cathy appeared horrified. "Oh, I can't fire Julie," she said. "Her husband and my husband work together, and we live in the same neighborhood and go to the same church. I can't fire her, because we see each other too much after work. Firing her would put a very uncomfortable strain on our relationship."

I didn't say anything, but that didn't mean I wasn't thinking of something I could say. But that's not important. Instead, we arrived at the office and I reviewed the records. Again, the solution to the problem seemed clear.

"Cathy," I said. "You've got to fire Julie."

"Oh, I can't fire Julie," Cathy repeated. "Her husband and my husband work together, and we live in the same neighborhood . . ."

Again, I kept my thoughts to myself, even though it hurt. Later, I staged a meeting with all the members of the sales force and was trying my best to establish a common cause to pull them together as a team. Nine of the ten-member force were really involved with my presentation. If they weren't actually verbally agreeing with my strategies, their faces, at least, showed their interest and budding enthusiasm.

Guess who was the lone holdout—the one who sat to my left with a stern look on her face while her deep sighs of discontent and boredom sounded throughout the room. That's right. It was Julie.

"Cathy," I said after the meeting. "You've just got to fire Julie. She is not only *not* for your cause, but she's going out of her way to be against it. Get rid of her."

"Oh, I can't fire Julie," Cathy said. "Her husband and my husband work together, and we live . . ."

In frustration, I dropped the topic and spent the remainder of my time in Newark doing what I could to reverse the slump. About two months later, I called Cathy to see if the slump had reversed itself.

"No," she said. "In fact, things are getting worse."

"Cathy," I said. "Did you fire Julie?"

"Oh, I can't fire Julie," Cathy said. "Her husband . . ."

That was it. I had heard it before, and I didn't need to hear it again. So I hung up the phone while she was in mid-sentence.

A few seconds later, my telephone rang. It was Cathy.

"Floyd," she said. "We must have been disconnected."

"No, we weren't," I said. "I hung up on you."

"Why?" Cathy asked.

"Because you're screwing up my reputation. I'm a consultant who sells his services by promising results and backing up my promise with a good track record, which you're screwing up!"

Then I told her again.

"Cathy," I said. "You've got to fire Julie. Until you do, the slump won't reverse itself, because you're sending the message to your sales team that poor performances and substandard production will be tolerated. There's only one way to reverse the trend—fire Julie!"

She did, finally. It wasn't long before what I predicted became reality. Production was on its way back up.

Of course, there will be some occasions when firing, at least right away, would be inappropriate, if not drastic. Perhaps what is necessary is a face-to-face, one-on-one meeting with your problem producer during which you discuss what it is about that person's performance that bothers you. Then you should communicate your expectations (that is, improved production) to the salesperson, along with your ultimatum (firing) if your expectations are not met.

Many managers ask me if there should be a time limit for the salesperson to achieve your expectations. Of course. Otherwise, the element of urgency to improve will be nonexistent, and the salesperson will have reduced motivation at best and none at worst to meet your expectations.

Of course, if the salesperson exceeds the time limit, then again, you have a choice to make. You either fire, or lower your standards.

STEP 3:
CALL A SPECIAL MEETING

Shortly after you fire the problem salesperson or salespeople, it will be necessary both from the standpoint of common courtesy and good business to inform the surviving members of the team. But don't fail to use this announcement to your best advantage in terms of making the strongest impression possible on your salespeople.

A "special" meeting is one that indicates that something in the works is different. To further convey this feeling, the meeting should be staged at an unusual time and an unusual place. Believe me, the mere announcement that a "special" meeting is to be held will make a difference in the attitudes of your employees.

It's important that this meeting be staged within hours after the non-productive salesperson was discharged, or else the effect you would like to create will be lost.

I once was approached by a sales manager who said, "Floyd,

I need to fire one of my salespeople, but I won't have time to stage a special meeting for a couple of weeks. What do I do?"

"Think about it," I said. "What should you do?"

The manager thought for about five seconds, then his face lit up like a light bulb. "I know," he said. "I won't fire the salesperson until the day I can stage the meeting."

Good thinking. I'll give the same advice to you: If you're planning on firing someone, don't do it until you have the time to stage a special meeting shortly after the person is discharged.

How many of your salespeople should be present for the meeting? All of them. That's imperative. You should send the message directly to all of your people so there will be no excuses for missing what is being said. Make this point non-negotiable, and make it clear that no-shows won't be tolerated.

If one of your salespeople flatly refuses to attend without excellent reason, then you have a decision to make: Either redesign your organizational chart to make that salesperson answerable to no one, or fire that salesperson, too. You've got to keep control, or you otherwise might as well fire yourself.

Don't let anyone convince you that one hundred percent attendance is impossible. I once agreed to stage three rallies free of charge for a group of offices on the condition that there was no less than 100 percent attendance at each; anything less and I walked out on the spot.

You know what I got for each of the three meetings? One hundred percent attendance. You can get it, too, provided that you make attendance mandatory. On the other hand, if you give your team the option not to attend, the majority of them will take that option. So don't give it to them.

The purpose of the meeting, of course, is to explain to your team why you fired your problem producer. Don't rip the dearly departed to shreds. You won't win any points for that, and it's unnecessary. You might even go so far as to point out the former salesperson's good qualities, if any.

But do state unequivocally the reason for discharging the salesperson. Perhaps you might address the situation by saying, "Gang, we have a team here, and (the discharged salesperson) just wasn't a team player. We need team players, because we're going to the moon, gang, and we've only got ten seats."

Then, you can launch into your "state of the company" address. Most of your salespeople will love hearing it; it should be the story of your company, from where it came, where it is now and where it's going. It's a good time to remind them that the company is thriving and will offer them a good chance of success.

Then, of course, you've got to make your team members understand a problem. What's the problem? The sales team must change its way of doing things, or the company goal may not be met.

You might vocalize it like this: "If we keep doing exactly what we're doing now, we're not going to hit our goal. The problem is, we're going to have to change. We're going to increase our productivity here by twenty-five percent. We have ten desks now, and the person sitting in your desk has to earn more. Mathematically, if we keep doing as well as we are now, in nine months and four days, we're going to be out of business.

"For us to grow, we've got to put together a better team, and all teams are only as good as their standards." Then, if your standards are insufficient for your company's needs, strengthen them. If your company has no minimum team activity standards listed, then you'd better devise some, because, with them, your company will make money easier and faster. It's a fact of business life.

The problem with which you must confront them is that they have never worked as a team because company standards have either been insufficient or non-existent. I believe if the salespeople are aware of the problem, they will come up with solutions. If salespeople know there must be rules, they'll devise the rules themselves. The same holds true with standards. If salespeople know there must be standards, they will come up with the standards.

Then you go to step four.

STEP 4: FISHBONING

Fishboning is one of the most powerful management tools there is, but like the six-step process in itself, this should not be overused. For optimum efficiency, treat this tool as a "secret weapon" of sorts. If it becomes standard fare, some or most of its impact will be lost. But if it's used sparingly, it can generate some very good ideas that won't cost you a cent and possibly will earn you plenty of dollars.

Fishboning is a brainstorming process that taps into the minds of your salespeople. It not only helps you to get solutions to your team's problems, but it also allows team members to participate in the decision-making process, provides recognition to people with good ideas, and the ideas often offer sympathetic help to the team itself. Remember, recognition, participation and sympathetic help are the three chief motivators of salespeople.

There are three rules to follow with fishboning to ensure that the process doesn't bog down in mid-session:

1. **Everyone must participate.** When it's a particular sales-person's time to speak, he or she must speak. No one is allowed to pass.

2. **There are no bad ideas.** Unlike brainstorming, no one is allowed to criticize ideas.

3. **Everyone writes everything down.** I recall in one fish-boning situation to determine why office morale was down, a relatively new agent said, "I haven't been here too long, but it seems to me that Don is always grumpy around here, so I feel like being grumpy, too." Under the rules of the game, Don cannot criticize; he can only

write down what was said—that Don is grumpy. Because
of this, fishboning is a great communication tool.

To set the stage for fishboning, create an informal atmosphere.
Everyone should sit in a circle. In cases where sales teams number
twenty or more people, more than one group should be formed;
under no circumstances should a group consist of more than twelve
people.

Select a moderator for each group. Make sure the person is
capable of leading the session; of course, you're the best judge of
that. Then have each person draw the following diagram on a blank
sheet of paper: a rectangle at the center with lines projecting outwardly
from the rectangle. How many lines? Two per participating salesperson.

If you really want to save your team members the hassle of
drawing straight lines, you may draw the diagram yourself and photo-
copy enough duplicates for your team members.

Then, it's time for you to identify the subject of the fishboning
process. The subjects could range from minimum team activities,
specific solutions to problems, methods of operation or to identify
a problem, such as why sales and/or morale is down.

Whatever topic is selected, each person in the group will be
asked to comment appropriately. For example, if sales are down,
each person would be asked to give his or her reason as to why.
Each person in the group should be solicited for his or her opinion.
Then, each person should be polled again, resulting in two opinions
per person.

Of course, everyone writes down everything that is being said.
The purpose behind the process is to make your team members
stretch their imaginations. If you're feeling particularly bold, you
might even ask each member for a third opinion. Sometimes, that's
where the results come. When you make team members stretch beyond
their "comfort zones," so to speak, their comments can be useful,
indeed.

Now if the team members never went beyond this step, you've

FISHBONING PROCESS

1. Identify objective (i.e. new team standards).

2. Go around the group clockwise or counter-clockwise and have each person come up with a possible team standard.

3. Discuss and vote democratically for agreed upon standards.

4 List top_____ agreed upon standards.

    1. _____

    2. _____

    3. _____

    4. _____

    5. _____

    6. _____

    7. _____

    8. _____

    9. _____

  10. _____

5. Each participant makes verbal commitment to adhere to top_____ standards at least established teamwork and cooperation. All of the team members are working on one problem, and all are participating. But the process continues. After the opinion phase of the process, there must be discussion of the best ideas. Of course, there may be some arguing between particular team members, and if there is, let them argue. As long as the discussion doesn't involve the swinging of fists and/or chairs, arguing can be healthy.

When the arguing is over, take a vote on the best ideas. How many of the best ideas you'd like to adopt, of course, is up to you. But the majority rules, and each individual team member should commit himself or herself to the majority's decision. (Refer to Diagram on page 217.)

STEP 5:
CREATE A COMMON CAUSE

It's important to unite your team with a specific purpose, and there are three good ways to do that. One is to challenge a foe, or competitor, within the marketplace. The best choice would be the competitor your salespeople most often discuss. The goal would be to beat the competition for a certain period of time.

Number two is to establish a new production goal. Achieving that goal might amount to setting a new company record. And number three would be an in-office contest. Now would be a good opportunity to kick off a contest as discussed in Strategy 12.

The point is, the common cause should unite your team members with a specific purpose, challenging them to work for a single cause that would, if achieved, benefit all. It takes teamwork to achieve a common goal.

STEP 6:
GET A COMMITMENT

Once the common cause has been established, each team member should make a commitment to stay on the team. They also should commit to any challenge that might be launched, as in the case of friendly competition among competitors. Finally and most importantly, every team member should sign an agreement to uphold the company's standards.

The commitment to remain on the team may be handled either in the group meeting or during a one-on-one session between salesperson and manager. The commitment to the challenge can be illustrated by a chart on the wall, with each salesperson's name and personal production statistics recorded for all salespeople to see.

But it's most important to have each team member sign an agreement, because psychologically, it inspires the person to persevere. As you well know yourself, perseverance is what it takes to succeed in the sales business.

IN A CAPSULE

1. There are three ways to upgrade a sales operation. Either set new goals, encourage personal and professional development or fire the problem salespeople.

2. A sales team is a sales manager's vehicle to success. It will serve the manager no better or worse than the attention he or she devotes to the team.

3. The six-step process to success should be used sparingly. It's a great tool to use to increase productivity when you reorganize or if you want to build a team from the ashes of ruin.

4. Step one of the six-step process is to rate each salesperson, along with yourself, in four categories: current perceived attitude, noticeable effort, current relative production and consistent use of company approved systems.

5. Step two involves firing (or at least issuing an ultimatum) to problem salespeople.

6. Step three involves staging a special meeting to inform the surviving salespeople of the firing.

7. Step four involves fishboning, or a communal talk session to solicit money-making ideas. Everyone must talk when it's his or her turn, and criticisms are not allowed.

8. Step five involves creating a common cause to unite team members. Either set a new company goal or stage a contest, either within the office or by challenging a competitor.

9. Step six involves getting from each team member in writing individual commitments to remain on the team. This inspires them to persevere.

List the most important points you have gained from the
preceding Strategy:

_____

_____

_____

_____

_____

_____

_____

_____

_____

_____

_____

_____

_____

_____

_____

_____

_____

Strategy 14:

Follow the Ten Commandments of Leadership

Think about your best friend for a moment. Why do you like him or her? I'll bet your answer will be similar to mine: I like my best friend because of the way that person makes me feel. I **like** and **respect** my best friend, and my best friend **likes** and **respects** me.

Good friends are considerate of and hold mutual respect for each other. They enjoy each other's company and will go out of their way to maintain their relationships. They would even "go to war" for each other, because they know that good friends are hard to find.

The same is true for good sales people. If you've ever lost one of your better producers, you know this already.

If people really **like** and **respect** you, they will stay with you longer, be happier at their jobs, perform better and—if they respect you enough—"go to war" for you when the business really needs a show of strength.

In fact, if people really **like** and **respect** you, they will even work for free for a short period of time to help accomplish a company goal or solve a serious problem. I really believe this, mainly because I've seen it happen time and time again.

Yet, whenever I sound this belief to an audience, most people react skeptically (judging by the audible groans and grunts that all too clearly signify the presence of doubt). But there are usually at least a few people present who remain silent, because they know what I'm talking about. Throughout my years of experience as a sales manager, I can recall many times when salespeople put in extra effort in exchange for reduced or no income at all to solve a business problem.

How do you motivate people to stay with you, work hard, increase production and be happy about it? How do you motivate an employee to "go to war" at great personal sacrifice? **The answer is simple: Get them to like and respect you.**

Based on my experience in the sales business, I believe that, given a choice, people would rather do work they don't particularly enjoy for people they **like** and **respect** than to do work they enjoy for people they despise. I believe that if you get people to **like** and **respect** you first, enjoyment of the job will follow. Treat your associates in a manner that will make them **like** and **respect** you, and you'll have a management-subordinate relationship that you and the salesperson will value to the bitter end.

So who do you think bears the burden of creating this relationship? That's right—you do. And it's important that you do it correctly.

You can make your associates do practically anything you'd like through negative "do-it-or-else" motivation (I don't recommend this; I'm just stating a fact). However, the first chance they get, they'll jump ship, and you'll be looking for someone else to kick around.

But you'll never make anyone like you through negative motivation. If an associate doesn't like you, he or she won't respect you and, as a result, will work below potential at best, and at worst, will turn in peak performance—for the competition.

No, you can't make someone **like** and **respect** you. But you *can* create an atmosphere conducive to mutual admiration and respect between you and your associates. I've found through my years of working with people—be it as a real estate agent, sales manager, trainer or keynote convention speaker—that by following a self-made list of guidelines for effective associate-manager interaction, admiration and respect are the natural results. These we'll call "The Ten Commandments."

So, in this chapter, I'd like to list my Ten Commandments of Leadership. When everything seems to be turning to sand, when your best people are leaving you and those who remain are not producing for you, when on-the-job happiness is only a memory and the call to battle gets little or no positive response, a good leader will know that he or she just might be a part of the problem.

Then, being the good leader that you are, you can refer to these Ten Commandments and determine if you can improve the situation by improving your leadership practices.

So let's examine **Floyd Wickman's** *Ten Commandments of Leadership.* I'm not going to say that if you subscribe to these management practices, you'll never have any more problems. But if you do, I think you'll find there will be few, if any, problems arising that can't be handled effectively and efficiently by you and your loyal team, which is exactly what you'll have at your disposal.

THE FIRST COMMANDMENT:
THOU SHALT ALWAYS CRITICIZE IN PRIVATE

I realize that keeping silent can sometimes be extremely difficult, especially when you see one of your salespeople fouling up at a time when the company can't stand any foul-ups. In the heat of such a moment, it's very tempting to chew out the salesperson on the spot.

Don't do it. First, to everyone present, you'll be the heavy. Regardless of the nature of the offense, people find it uncomfortable and embarrassing to watch a manager berate a subordinate. Second—and most importantly—it's demeaning to the salesperson. Consequently, he or she at that very moment will like you less than he or she did a minute earlier. When your people stop liking you, guess what—they stop respecting you, too.

Let me give you an example: Sam Schwartz makes a sale—his first in eight weeks. He walks into the office feeling like a million bucks and announces with new-found confidence, "I made a sale!"

At this point, the manager gets up out of his chair and, with an incredulous look on his face, checks out the contract. Suddenly, the manager's face contorts in anger as he or she slams down the document on a nearby desk.

"Sam, you idiot, what are you doing?" the manager shouts loudly enough to command the attention of everyone in the building. "This could have been a good sale, but, holy cow, you cut the unit price by 10 percent! Heck, you didn't have to do that. You could have held firm and got the customer to pay full price!"

What do you think is happening with Sam at that moment? To say the least, Sam doesn't feel good anymore. To be more specific, Sam likes the boss at that moment just a little less than he did a minute earlier. Sam, at that moment, surely respects the manager a little less.

But more importantly is the future effect the public scolding will have on Sam. I can tell you from experience that Sam, after being humiliated before his peers, will not put himself out any more than is absolutely necessary to keep his job. Consequently, he will be a little less productive because he'll be a little more apprehensive to bring in a sale for fear it will be held up as a poor example for all of his peers to see.

Now don't get me wrong. Criticism sometimes is necessary,

provided that it's done properly and privately. It's only through constructive criticism that we as individuals can grow. In fact, you can say virtually anything you want in private, and the salesperson will listen. But when criticism is used as a management weapon to embarrass or demean, it becomes a destructive weapon that very often will cost its user dearly.

So remember, if you are going to criticize your people, do it in private.

THE SECOND COMMANDMENT:
THOU SHALT ALWAYS PRAISE IN PUBLIC

If public criticism is demeaning, what effect do you think public praising will have on the associate? When people are praised before their peers, their confidence will soar.

If you have praises or compliments for a salesperson, always go out of your way to let as many people as possible know that you are proud. In fact, it wouldn't hurt to advertise it. I'm serious. The insurance, real estate and automobile industries do this regularly. I'll bet that you can't find a local daily newspaper anywhere in North America today that doesn't include at least one picture of a salesperson, along with a corporate boast that he or she was sales leader of the month, top producer for the quarter, award winner for the year or some kind of record setter in the industry. It's a great way to publicize the business and publicly praise the employee at the same time.

When your salespeople know that you are proud enough of their accomplishments to advertise them, they will respect you more, stay with you longer and be happier and more productive while they are there. More importantly, they'll be far more eager to take up your cause when you need them to "go to war" than salespeople who are dressed down in public.

So when you have something nice to say about one of your salespeople, always go out of your way to say it where the most ears can hear it.

THE THIRD COMMANDMENT:
THOU SHALT LET THY SALESPEOPLE BE INDEPENDENT OF YOU

People have a tendency to love and respect their trusted psychiatrists, psychoanalysts and counselors. In fact, they have a tendency to love and respect them so much that they are quite happy during their visits. They look forward to their visits, they produce whatever they are told to produce and, at certain times, might even go to war for the shrink. A real love relationship is developed.

Of course, all this is common knowledge. But what a lot of people don't understand is why this relationship is formed. Actually, it occurs because we are all tall kids. All of us are whatever we were way back when we were two years old. Somehow, you never get away from that. Furthermore, we'd all be practically as helpless as we were at two years of age had our parents not taught us how to do things for ourselves. When parents allow us to be independent of them, we have a great deal more admiration for them than if they spare us the trouble of growing up by always doing for us.

It's been my experience to discover that the same holds true in the business world. If you help salespeople become independent, you'll be giving them something that will never go away. They not only become better salespeople, but they become better people as well.

How do you make salespeople independent of you rather than dependent upon you? We covered this in a previous chapter in the training section. However, the rules are simple enough to repeat:

228

simply give them the job, explain the rules, state the desired end result and then let them do it. That's it. If they make a mistake, lift them up and have them start again until they can do it right. Don't be too quick to dive in and do it for them.

Again, I believe that when people feel you've let them become independent of you, they will like you better, will respect you more and, as a result, stay longer than they otherwise might. They will be happy at what they do, they will produce more for you and, at those times when you need it, they will go to war for you.

THE FOURTH COMMANDMENT:
THOU SHALT BE A BOSS, NOT A BUDDY

Sometimes, it's possible for managers and their salespeople to get "too close," or get on each other's nerves. Everyone has heard the adage, "Familiarity breeds contempt." Well, I take minor issue. I believe that familiarity can breed contempt, but it doesn't always. However, the closer you are to someone, the more you show your real self. As a result, personal weaknesses often surface.

When salespeople feel that they are buddies with the boss, they become harder to manage. For example, a sales manager and a salesperson go out for an evening.

Let me make it clear that I think socializing with salespeople is fine—to a point. There's nothing wrong with a manager and a subordinate having dinner and a couple of drinks, attending a sports event, the theater or whatever activity they find appealing.

However, I believe that this sort of thing can definitely be overdone. If you go out too often, stay too long or drink too much, there is a good chance that the manager and subordinate will cease being Mr. Smith and Mary or Ms. Smith and Jack and suddenly will become Tom and Mary or Susan and Jack. After a few more drinks, words will start to slur, and soon, Mary or Jack will be giving manager Tom or Susan advice on how the sales division should be run.

If you ever find yourself in this situation, your weaknesses likely will show. Your salespeople will notice them and, as a result, will respect you a little less. Don't get me wrong, they might think you're the greatest person since the beginning of time, but they will still respect you less as a manager. In this relationship, this is your first and foremost responsibility.

Remember, if your salespeople respect you less, they won't stay with you as long, and they won't be as happy nor will they produce as much while they're there. Furthermore, forget about offering them advice. There's a good chance that they'll argue with you. They'll fight you when you need them to join you. Why? Because you have become their buddy, and buddies can say anything they want to each other.

So remember, don't be a buddy. Be a boss. Everyone will be much happier in the long run.

THE FIFTH COMMANDMENT:
THOU SHALT LET THY SALESPEOPLE PARTICIPATE

It goes without saying that one of the main reasons some people are dissatisfied with their jobs is they feel that no one in management cares about their input.

Put yourself in their shoes. You're a salesperson who is investing a lot of effort and energy into the company, and you've got ideas. Yet, the company doesn't seem to be at all interested in your input. The sales manager never seeks your advice, nor does he or she allow you to participate in the planning, decision-making or problem solving processes. Under those circumstances, how would you feel about the company?

Of course, you might stay there because the money is right, but you won't necessarily respect the company's philosophy. Furthermore, I'll bet you'd jump ship at the first better opportunity that arose.

This same principle holds true on a one-to-one basis. Your salespeople will respect you if you allow them a voice in matters that concern them. Salespeople always want to throw in their two cents' worth, and sometimes, it can amount to big bucks for the company.

Permit your salespeople to participate by giving them a project and asking them to provide you with their solutions before you make a final decision. This will build confidence and self-esteem among the ranks. When salespeople can participate in company functions—even some that might be at a higher level than their job description involves—they'll feel more a part of the company. As a result, they will respect you more, stay with you longer, and they'll be happier and produce more while they're there. Furthermore, when you need your salespeople to be soldiers of "war," you'll have a band of willing volunteers at your disposal.

THE SIXTH COMMANDMENT:
THOU SHALT SERVE AS FINE EXAMPLE

I've learned this one, time and time again, through painful experience. Many times when, as a sales manager, I would notice that my team's morale was particularly low, I'd spend weeks trying to find out why. Finally, it would dawn on me that I was probably at least part of the problem by setting a bad example. For whatever reason, my morale would be low, and my team would follow suit.

If you want your people to be cheerful, it's got to start with you. Any parent reading this book knows that children are more heavily influenced by what we do than by what we say. We can talk until we're blue in the face, but they will follow our example every time.

As I've mentioned many times in this book, we're all tall kids. If sales managers set good examples, salespeople will react accordingly. Examples can include a nice appearance, a positive attitude, even temperament, hard work and increased productivity.

If your salespeople see that you practice more than preach, they'll respect you for it. People respect leaders who aren't above doing what they tell their salespeople to do. On the other hand, salespeople tend to disrespect leaders who feel they're above their own directives.

Leaders must remember this commandment often. Those who are inclined to think this commandment doesn't apply to them will pay a dear price later because, within a relatively short period of time, their teams will follow the managers' examples.

THE SEVENTH COMMANDMENT:
THOU SHALT BE A GOOD COMMUNICATOR

The subject of communication could easily fill numerous volumes of books, but I only want to deal with a few categories of communication as they apply to the everyday business world, especially the sales business.

The first category is listening. Listen to your people. Encourage them to say what's on their minds. Allow them the opportunity and the freedom to come into your office and complain about you, about a company procedure, policy or method, or any phase of the business in general. Let them know that, at times, they can "dump on you."

This is best accomplished through an "open-door" policy. One of the best managers I have ever met in the real estate business completely turned his team morale around 180 degrees (in the positive direction) by using one of the simplest, yet one of the most powerful, tricks in the book. He noticed that morale and production were down. His salespeople seemed to be fragmented into little cliques, and team spirit, of course, was suffering.

After attending a management program where the subject of effective communication was discussed, he started analyzing the problem and found that he was part of it. He realized that although he was there all the time, the only time he really spent with his salespeople was when he was criticizing them or attending a previously planned meeting.

So the next Monday morning, he walked into his office with a screwdriver and proceeded to take his office door off its hinges. Without saying a word, he carried the door to the company storage room, and it has been there ever since. Then he announced that, from that point on, an open-door policy would be in effect. Anyone with anything to say to him had only to walk into his office. There was no longer a door in the way. As a result, morale miraculously— and immediately—improved, because the salespeople gained additional respect for their manager.

The second area of effective communication is effective delivery of your expectations to others. In short, lay it all out up front, and don't beat around the bush. Good communicators make extremely clear their expectations and allow their salespeople to do the same.

Turnover in the sales business is atrocious and that could be cut down a great deal if people would communicate expectations up front. In the social world, the divorce rate is atrocious. I've seen statistics which indicate that one out of every two marriages today will fail. I can't help but believe that good communication could help reduce the divorce rate. If engaged people would communicate their expectations up front before saying "I do," they would have a more realistic idea of what to expect from each other. The same applies for manager-salesperson relationships.

The third area of effective communication in business is keeping salespeople informed of new policies or procedures that might affect them. Salespeople will respect you more if you don't keep them in the dark. When you get word of a change that affects your salespeople, it will be to your advantage to let your team know about it as soon as possible. If there is a change in unit price, market conditions or financing arrangements, let your salespeople know.

So, in a nutshell, listen to your salespeople, be up front with them and keep them informed. It's very important for leaders to maintain a very strong information system. If salespeople know they'll be the first to know of changes that affect them, they will feel more important to the company and, as a result, respect you more for keeping them clued.

THE EIGHTH COMMANDMENT:
THOU SHALT TRUST YOUR SALESPEOPLE

Trust is a risky business. Some sales managers I've met trust none of their salespeople until their salespeople prove they are worthy of their trust. Of course, this often results in a Mexican stand-off. After all, if a manager can only trust a salesperson after he or she proves trustworthy, then the manager really isn't trusting the salesperson at all.

Effective sales managers give their salespeople some up-front blind faith. Rather than withholding trust until the salesperson proves trustworthy, effective sales managers trust their salespeople until they prove they can't be trusted.

I apologize for making a personal reference here, but when I think of trust, I always think of my three sons—my own, that is, not the once popular television series. I have three sons who are young men now. But the whole time they were growing up, they gave my wife Linda and me absolutely zero problems. I want to say that again—zero problems! There was no trouble with the police, no trouble with drugs and no trouble with school.

If I do say so myself, I think that's amazing, considering the fact that they have lived a unique lifestyle. Being a salesman, sales manager and professional sales trainer and speaker, I have been home very seldom during the past fifteen years. Instead, I have been flying around North America practically on a daily basis. Sometimes, Linda would be with me. When I wasn't working, Linda and I left the boys at home quite often while we took mini-vacations. Still, there was never any trouble.

Occasionally, Linda and I will take a break, have a glass of wine and sit down before a crackling fire in the family room and talk about how well our children turned out. I used to think that we were just lucky until one day Linda put things in perspective.

"I don't think it was luck that our kids grew up so well," she said. "I think it was because we trusted them."

"Why shouldn't we have trusted them? They never gave us any reason not to trust them," I responded.

"No, the trust came first. If you trust your children, they will go out of their way to prove you're right. If you don't trust them, they will go out of their way to prove you're right," she concluded.

It's the same way with managing salespeople, and I've used Linda's line about trust many times in management seminars. It's just another way of saying that salespeople will live up or down to your expectations.

Bearing that in mind, I'd say a little unconditional trust up front can go a long way toward building the type of sales team your competition would love to steal. But you won't have to worry about them leaving, because if you trust them, they'll respect you more, stay with you longer and be happier and more productive while they're there. Furthermore, a trusted soul will "go to war" more willingly than one who isn't trusted.

THE NINTH COMMANDMENT:
THOU SHALT SHOW THAT YOU CARE

Salespeople are great for showing that they care about their clients. They'll go out of their way to write a thank-you note, send flowers or take their clients out to lunch or dinner. But, of course, there is an ulterior motive—to get future business.

But how about within the organization? It's been my experience that when it comes to showing concern for their salespeople, most sales managers are sadly deficient.

You can't merely assume that your salespeople automatically know that you care. I think you have to go out of your way to show them that you care, and there are some very simple ways to do this. A hug or handshake with a few words of appreciation is nice. Better yet, you can send them flowers, a bottle of wine or give them the afternoon off when they least expect it. Of course, you can use your own imagination with the various individuals on your team to come up with other ways of showing that you care.

Many times, when sales managers show they care about their salespeople, they are actually filling voids in their salespeople's lives. Why? Because many of those salespeople aren't getting that kind of attention elsewhere. But, under any circumstances, your salespeople will care more for you and will respect you more if you're the type of person who shows that you care about them as people, not just as employees.

THE TENTH COMMANDMENT:
THOU SHALT WORK AS A TEAM

A team is a group of people working together, as opposed to a group of people subdivided, departmentalized and sectioned off. Un-

236

der such conditions, the proverbial right hand not only doesn't know what the left hand is doing—it doesn't care, because it's not the right hand's job to care.

Teamwork is the concept of various departments and divisions working together toward common causes. You can develop a team applying each and every one of the management principles we've covered in this book. However, I made teamwork the final commandment because people working together toward a common cause is the essence of maximum productivity, or the quickest way to get where you're going.

What is the quickest way to get there? The quickest way "to get there" is "together." A strong team is an asset to any sales operation, and that includes your company, too.

IN CONCLUSION

I believe that if you follow these Ten Commandments of Leadership, you'll have little problem managing a strong team of capable, committed individuals who will be as loyal as they'll be effective.

Of course, how many of you can cite each one of the real Ten Commandments? If you can't, I feel it's safe to say that you might forget my Ten Commandments as well. Even though we often know how we should behave as sales managers, sometimes it's easy to forget.

Therefore, at the back of this book, these Ten Commandments are printed. If you remind yourself of these guidelines every day, you'll find yourself practicing them consistently, which is what it takes to build a consistently effective team.

Then, you'll find out (if you don't know already) what it's like to lead a team of individuals who **like** and **respect** you, who will stay with you longer than average, who will be happier and produce more while they're there and who, should the time ever come, will go to war for you when you need them most.

And if that should happen, odds are good that you'll be fighting a battle that you'll win.

IN A CAPSULE

1. The First Commandment: Thou Shalt Always Criticize In Private.

2. The Second Commandment: Thou Shalt Always Praise In Public.

3. The Third Commandment: Thou Shalt Let Thy Salespeople Be Independent Of You.

4. The Fourth Commandment: Thou Shalt Be A Boss, Not A Buddy.

5. The Fifth Commandment: Thou Shalt Let Thy Salespeople Participate.

6. The Sixth Commandment: Thou Shalt Serve As Fine Example.

7. The Seventh Commandment: Thou Shalt Be A Good Communicator.

8. The Eighth Commandment: Thou Shalt Trust Your Salespeople.

9. The Ninth Commandment: Thou Shalt Show That You Care.

10. The Tenth Commandment: Thou Shalt Work As A Team.

List the most important points you have gained from the
preceding Strategy:

_____

_____

_____

_____

_____

_____

_____

_____

_____

_____

_____

_____

_____

_____

_____

_____

_____

NOTES

Epilogue

Now that you've read this book, I hope you'll be motivated to bring out the best in your sales team. If you don't, they'll wind up getting the best of you. That's a promise.

Remember, fun is the key. Successful salespeople are successful because they have fun. Turn their jobs into drudgeries and both you and your salespeople will suffer.

Manage your team by having fun. You'll have better results and fewer headaches than the sales manager who thinks that fun is only for kids and that salespeople should always conduct themselves in a solemn, serious fashion.

Now I'm not saying that selling is not serious business. It is indeed a sophisticated business, especially in this day and age. It's also a competitive business, considering the number of competitors in any given field. Now, more than ever, it's important that your sales team move in the right direction in the least amount of time for the most positive results.

Lead your sales team to success. With these principles, you can do it. Since your income depends either directly or indirectly upon their production, you'll share in the rewards, not to mention the fact that your company will benefit accordingly. Everybody will win!

This should be good news to your salespeople and company officials alike. Good luck, and, by all means, have fun!

FLOYD WICKMAN'S "TEN COMMANDMENTS OF LEADERSHIP"

The First Commandment
Thou Shalt Always Criticize In Private.

The Second Commandment
Thou Shalt Always Praise In Public.

The Third Commandment
Thou Shalt Let Thy Salespeople Be Independent Of You.

The Fourth Commandment
Thou Shalt Be A Boss, Not A Buddy.

The Fifth Commandment
Thou Shalt Let Thy Salespeople Participate.

The Sixth Commandment
Thou Shalt Serve As Fine Example.

The Seventh Commandment
Thou Shalt Be A Good Communicator.

The Eighth Commandment
Thou Shalt Trust Your Salespeople.

The Ninth Commandment
Thou Shalt Show That You Care.

The Tenth Commandment
Thou Shalt Work As A Team.

For Further
Information

For information on Floyd Wickman's availability to speak at your next seminar, rally, or convention, or for questions regarding this book or other Floyd Wickman products, write Floyd Wickman and Associates, 2119 East Fourteen Mile Road, Sterling Heights, Michigan 48310 or call (313) 978-1900.